How To Become an EV Technician

RONIN C. ABEL

ISBN: 9798868134067

DEDICATION

I proudly dedicate this work to my three charming grandniece
and grandnephews – Natalia, Davian and Andre.

CONTENTS

1   Introduction   1

2   Getting Started   Pg 8

3   EV Fundamentals   Pg 42

4   EV Safety   Pg 58

5   EV Maintenance and Repair   Pg 76

6   Advanced EV Topics   Pg 99

7   Career Advancements   Pg 118

8   Conclusion   Pg 139

AUTHOR'S DISCLAIMER

This book is intended to provide general information and guidance on the skills and knowledge required to become an EV service technician. It is not a substitute for professional advice or training from a qualified instructor or institution. The author and publisher have made every effort to ensure the accuracy and completeness of the information contained in this book, but they do not guarantee or warrant that it is error-free, up-to-date, or applicable to every situation.

The reader is responsible for verifying the information before relying on it and for complying with all relevant laws, regulations, standards, and codes of practice. The author and publisher disclaim any liability for any loss, damage, injury, or expense that may result from the use or misuse of the information in this book.

1 INTRODUCTION

Electric vehicles (EVs) are the future of transportation. As more and more people switch to EVs, there will be a growing need for qualified EV service technicians. This book will provide you with the information and resources you need to become an EV technician. We will cover everything from the basics of automotive mechanics to the latest EV technologies. We will also provide you with tips on how to find an apprenticeship or job and how to advance your career.

EV technicians are responsible for the maintenance and repair of electric vehicles. They work on a variety of EV components, including batteries, motors, and charging systems. EV technicians must have a strong understanding of electricity and electronics, as well as the specific systems used in EVs.

There are several ways to become an EV service technician. One option is to complete an apprenticeship program. Apprenticeship programs typically last two to four years and combine classroom instruction with on-the-job training. Another option is to earn a degree in automotive technology or a related field. Many colleges and universities offer programs that specialize in EV technology.

If you are passionate about the auto industry and want to help shape the future of transportation, becoming an EV technician is a good career choice. Opportunities abound in both the public and private sectors. EV technicians can work for dealerships, repair shops, and manufacturers. Once you have the necessary education and training, you can start looking for a job as an EV service technician.

What is an EV Technician?

So, what is an EV technician? An EV technician is a professional who specializes in diagnosing, servicing and repairing electric vehicles and charging stations. EV technicians work with high-voltage systems, batteries, motors, controllers and other components of electric vehicles. They may also install, design and maintain residential or commercial charging stations for electric vehicles.

EV technicians play an important role in keeping EVs running safely and efficiently. They are in high demand and earn competitive salaries. They can work on cutting-edge technology and help to reduce the environmental impact of transportation.

What Does an EV Technician Do?

An EV technician performs various tasks related to electric vehicles. Some of the common duties of an EV technician are:

• Diagnosing and troubleshooting problems with electric vehicles, such as battery degradation, motor failure, controller malfunction, etc.

• Performing routine maintenance and repairs on electric vehicles, such as replacing fluids, filters, brakes, tires, etc.

• Testing and calibrating electric vehicle systems and components, such as voltage, current, power, efficiency, etc.

• Installing and configuring new or upgraded electric vehicle parts and accessories, such as software updates, sensors, cameras, etc.

- Designing and installing charging stations for electric vehicles, such as selecting the location, wiring, circuit breakers, connectors, etc.
- Maintaining and servicing charging stations for electric vehicles, such as cleaning, inspecting, repairing, etc.
- Educating customers and clients about electric vehicles and charging stations, such as explaining the features, benefits, safety precautions, etc.

In addition to the above, an EV technician may also need to have some skills and knowledge in areas such as electrical and electronic engineering, automotive mechanics, computer programming, customer service, and safety regulations.

Anyone who wants to become an EV technician should have a strong interest in cars and automotive technology. You should also be able to work independently and as part of a team. And you should also be willing to learn new things as EV technology is constantly evolving.

Why Become an EV Technician?

There are many reasons why a person like you might want to become an EV technician. Here are a few good reasons to think about:

- Job security: The EV market is growing rapidly, and there is a high demand for qualified EV technicians. As more and more people switch to EVs, the need for EV technicians will continue to grow.

- Competitive salary: EV technicians typically earn competitive salaries. The median annual salary for automotive technicians was $48,560 in 2021, according to the Bureau of Labor Statistics. EV technicians typically earn more than the median salary for automotive technicians.

- Rewarding work: EV technicians play an important role in helping people to reduce their carbon footprint and save money on gas. It's a great feeling to know that you're making a difference for the environment and for your customers.

- Opportunity to learn cutting-edge technology: EVs are complex machines, and EV technicians need to have a strong understanding of electricity, electronics, and automotive technology. EV technicians are constantly learning new things, as EV technology is constantly evolving.

There are many opportunities for EV technicians to advance their careers, such as becoming a lead technician, service manager, or even starting their own business. If you're considering a career as an EV technician, I encourage you to learn more about the field and explore your options. There are many resources available to help you get started, such as online courses, apprenticeship programs, and certification programs.

Job Outlook for EV Technicians

The job outlook for EV technicians is very positive. The Bureau of Labor Statistics projects that employment of automotive service technicians and mechanics, which includes EV technicians, will grow 2 percent from 2022 to 2032, about as fast as the average for all occupations. About 67,700 openings for automotive service technicians and mechanics are projected each year, on average, over the decade.

The growth in demand for EV technicians is being driven by the increasing popularity of electric vehicles. As more and more people switch to EVs, there is a growing need for qualified EV technicians. In addition, the government and the automotive industry are investing heavily in the development and deployment of EV infrastructure. This investment is creating new jobs for EV technicians in the areas of EV charging station installation and maintenance.

Some of the factors contributing to the strong job

outlook for EV technicians include:

- The increasing popularity of electric vehicles
- Government and industry investment in EV infrastructure
- The growing number of EVs on the road
- The aging workforce of automotive technicians

If you choose EV technician as a career, then consider the following points to help improve your chances of finding a job:

- Get an education in automotive technology or a related field. Many community colleges and technical schools offer programs in automotive technology.
- Complete an apprenticeship program. Apprenticeships allow you to learn from experienced EV technicians while you earn a paycheck.
- Get certified as an EV technician. There are a number of organizations that offer EV technician certifications.

Becoming an EV technician is a great way to combine your love of cars with your desire to make a difference in the world. In the next chapter, we will explore the steps you should take as you embark on a journey to becoming an EV service technician.

2 GETTING STARTED

There are a number of rewards that come with being an EV technician. For example, EV technicians often get to work on the latest and greatest EV technology. They also have the opportunity to interact with customers and help them learn about and maintain their EVs. And, because the EV industry is relatively new, there are many opportunities for technicians to advance their careers and take on leadership roles.

In this chapter, we will consider some of the fundamentals for getting started on the path to becoming an EV technician. We will take a close look at:

- Education and training requirements
- Finding an apprenticeship or job

- Tools and equipment you will need

Let's begin by looking at the educational and training requirements for becoming an EV technician.

EDUCATION AND TRAINING REQUIREMENTS

What are the basic education and training requirements for becoming an EV technician? The answer is not so simple as it depends on the employer and the specific job duties. However, most employers require EV technicians to have at least a high school diploma or equivalent. Many employers also prefer EV technicians to have some postsecondary education, such as a certificate or associate's degree in automotive technology.

An EV technician training programs typically cover topics such as:
- EV basics
- EV system components
- EV diagnosis and repair
- EV safety
- EV charging and infrastructure

Some EV technician training programs offer specialization in areas such as high-voltage systems, batteries, or charging infrastructure.

In addition to formal education and training, it is also important for EV technicians to have hands-on experience. Many EV technicians gain experience by working as apprentices at EV repair shops or dealerships.

Once you have the necessary education, training, and experience, you may want to consider getting certified as an EV technician. There are a number of organizations that offer EV technician certification programs, such as the National Institute for Automotive Service Excellence (ASE). Getting certified can demonstrate your skills to potential employers and help you advance your career.

Here is a summary of the educational requirements for becoming an EV technician:
- Education: High school diploma or equivalent; postsecondary education (certificate or associate's degree in automotive technology) preferred
- Training: EV technician training program at a community college or vocational school

- Experience: Apprenticeship or entry-level job at an EV repair shop or dealership
- Certification: Optional, but recommended

Which Type of Program is Right for You?

The best type of EV technician training program for you depends on your individual needs and learning style. If you are looking for a program that offers hands-on training and instructor interaction, then an in-person program may be a good option for you. If you are looking for a program that is flexible and affordable, then an online program may be a good option for you.

The best way to decide which type of program is right for you is to research different programs and compare their features and benefits. You should also consider your own learning style and preferences.

Online

An online EV technician training program typically consists of a combination of video lectures, interactive exercises, and hands-on projects. Students can typically access the program materials at any time and from any location with an internet connection.

The curriculum for an online EV technician

training program typically covers topics such as:

- EV basics
- EV system components
- EV diagnosis and repair
- EV safety
- EV charging and infrastructure

In addition to the core curriculum, many online EV technician training programs also offer students the opportunity to complete hands-on projects. These projects can help students to gain practical experience working with EVs.

Advantages:

Online EV technician training programs offer the following advantages:

- Flexibility: Online programs offer students more flexibility than in-person programs. Students can typically complete online programs at their own pace and on their own schedule.
- Cost: Online programs are typically less expensive than in-person programs.
- Convenience: Online programs can be completed from anywhere in the world, as long as students have access to a computer and an internet connection.

<u>Disadvantages</u>:

• Lack of hands-on training: Online programs typically focus on theoretical knowledge, which is important, but it is not enough to become a competent EV technician. Hands-on training is essential for learning how to diagnose and repair EV components and systems.

• Limited access to equipment: Online programs do not typically provide students with access to EV equipment, which can make it difficult to practice what they are learning. Students may need to find their own EV to practice on, or they may need to enroll in a hybrid program that combines online instruction with hands-on training at a physical location.

• Lack of support from instructors: Online students may have difficulty getting support from their instructors, especially if they are struggling with a particular concept or skill. It can be helpful to choose an online program with a good reputation and a track record of providing support to students.

Students can typically complete an online EV technician training program in a few months to a year, depending on the program's length and the student's pace. Once students have completed an online EV technician training program, they may be eligible to take and pass an EV technician certification exam.

In-Person

An in-person EV technician training program typically consists of a combination of lectures, demonstrations, and hands-on training. Students can typically attend the program on a full-time or part-time basis.

The curriculum for an in-person EV technician training program typically covers topics such as:

- EV basics
- EV system components
- EV diagnosis and repair
- EV safety
- EV charging and infrastructure

In addition to the core curriculum, many in-person EV technician training programs also offer students the opportunity to complete internships or apprenticeships. Internships and apprenticeships can help students to gain practical experience working with EVs.

Advantages:
In-person EV technician training programs offer

the following advantages:

• Hands-on training: In-person programs typically offer more hands-on training than online programs. This is important because EV technicians need to be able to diagnose and repair EVs using specialized tools and equipment.

• Instructor interaction: In-person programs allow students to interact with their instructors in real time. This can be helpful for students who need extra help with certain concepts or who want to ask questions about the material.

• Lab access: In-person programs typically have access to labs where students can practice diagnosing and repairing EVs. This is important because it allows students to gain hands-on experience working with EVs in a safe and controlled environment.

Disadvantages:

• Cost: In-person training programs can be expensive, especially if they are offered by a private training provider. Students may need to pay for tuition, fees, and living expenses while they are attending the program.

• Time commitment: In-person training programs typically require students to attend classes on a full-time basis. This can be difficult for students who have other commitments, such as a job or family.

• Location: In-person training programs are typically offered in a specific location. This can be inconvenient for students who live far away from the training center.

• Lack of flexibility: In-person training programs typically have a set schedule that students must follow. This can be difficult for students who have other commitments or who need to take breaks for personal reasons.

Hands-On Experience

Hands-on experience is essential for EV technicians. It allows them to learn how to diagnose and repair EV components and systems safely and effectively. There are a number of ways for EV technicians to get hands-on experience, including:

• Enroll in a training program: Many EV technician training programs include hands-on training as part of the curriculum. These programs may provide students with access to EV equipment, such as vehicles, batteries, and motors.

• Get an internship or apprenticeship: Internships and apprenticeships can provide EV technicians with the opportunity to work on real-world EV projects under the supervision of experienced technicians.

- Volunteer at an EV repair shop: Many EV repair shops are willing to take on volunteers. This can be a great way for EV technicians to gain hands-on experience and learn from experienced technicians.

- Join an EV club or organization: There are a number of EV clubs and organizations that offer opportunities for EV technicians to get hands-on experience. These organizations may host events where EV technicians can work on vehicles, or they may provide access to EV equipment.

Here are some recommendations for getting the most out of a hands-on EV training:

- Be proactive and ask questions. Don't be afraid to ask your instructors or supervisors for help or clarification.

- Take notes and document your experience. This will help you to learn from your mistakes and to remember what you have learned.

- Be organized and efficient. This will help you to make the most of your time and to get the most out of your training.

- Be patient and don't get discouraged. It takes time and practice to become a skilled EV technician.

Scholarships

There are a number of scholarships available for EV technicians. Some of these scholarships are offered by government agencies, while others are offered by private organizations. Here are a few examples:

• TechForce Foundation Scholarships: The TechForce Foundation offers a number of scholarships for EV technicians, including the EV Opportunity Scholarship and the Electric Vehicle Technician Scholarship.

• National Institute for Automotive Service Excellence (ASE) Scholarships: The ASE offers a number of scholarships for students who are pursuing a career in automotive technology, including the ASE EV Specialist Scholarship.

• Society of Automotive Engineers (SAE) Scholarships: The SAE offers a number of scholarships for students who are pursuing a career in engineering, including the SAE Electric Vehicle Scholarship.

• Michigander EV & Mobility Tech Scholars: This scholarship is offered to Michigan Tech junior and senior-level students majoring in Software Engineering, Computer Science, Cybersecurity, Computer Network and System Administration, Electrical Engineering, Computer Engineering, and related programs.

- University of Hawaii Foundation Auto Tech Scholarships: These scholarships are offered to Hawaii residents who are enrolled in an automotive technology program at a University of Hawaii campus.

There are a number of other scholarships available for EV technicians. Students should search online and contact their local community college or university to learn more about scholarship opportunities.

Here are some suggestions for applying for EV technician scholarships:

- Start early. Many scholarship applications have deadlines that are months in advance.
- Be prepared to submit transcripts, letters of recommendation, and personal essays.
- Tailor your application to each scholarship. Be sure to highlight your skills and experience that are relevant to the scholarship.
- Proofread your application carefully before submitting it.

By following these tips, students can increase their chances of winning an EV technician scholarship.

Next, we will look at how to find an EV apprentice job.

FINDING AN EV APPRENTICESHIP JOB

What is an apprenticeship? An apprenticeship job is a paid job where you learn a skilled trade or profession through on-the-job training and classroom instruction. Apprenticeships typically last for one to four years, depending on the occupation. During this time, apprentices work under the supervision of experienced workers, who teach them the skills they need to succeed in their chosen field. Apprentices also complete classroom instruction to learn the theoretical aspects of their trade.

An EV apprenticeship job is a paid job where you learn the skills and knowledge needed to work on electric vehicles (EVs). This includes learning about the different components of EVs, how to diagnose and repair problems, and how to safely maintain them. EV apprentices also learn about the latest EV technologies and trends.

EV apprenticeship jobs typically last for one to four years, depending on the program. During this time, apprentices work under the supervision of experienced EV technicians. Apprentices learn by observing and assisting the technicians, and by completing hands-on training exercises. Apprentices also attend classroom instruction to learn the theoretical aspects of EV repair and maintenance.

Here are some of the tasks that an EV apprentice might perform:

• Assisting EV technicians with repairs and maintenance, such as replacing EV batteries or diagnosing electrical problems.

• Performing hands-on training exercises, such as learning how to use EV diagnostic tools or how to safely work with high-voltage electrical systems.

• Attending classroom instruction to learn about EV theory and technology, such as the different types of EV motors and batteries, or how to troubleshoot EV charging systems.

• Studying for and taking apprenticeship exams.

Upon completion of an EV apprenticeship program, apprentices earn a nationally recognized credential, such as an EV technician certificate or associate's degree. This credential can make them more competitive in the job market. If you are interested in an EV apprenticeship, you can search for programs in your area online or through your local career center.

There are a few different ways to find an EV apprenticeship:

•	Search online: There are a number of websites that list EV apprenticeship programs, such as the US Department of Labor's Apprenticeship.gov website and the National Electric Vehicle Infrastructure Training Program (NEVI) website.

•	Contact your local EV dealership or repair shop: Many EV dealerships and repair shops offer apprenticeship programs. You can contact them to inquire about their programs and how to apply.

•	Contact your local community college or trade school: Many community colleges and trade schools offer EV apprenticeship programs. You can contact them to inquire about their programs and how to apply.

•	Contact your local labor union: Some labor unions, such as the International Brotherhood of Electrical Workers (IBEW), offer EV apprenticeship programs. You can contact your local labor union to inquire about their programs and how to apply. You will typically need to submit an application, provide transcripts and references, and pass an interview.

Once you have found some EV apprenticeship

programs that you are interested in, you should contact the program sponsors to learn more about the programs and how to apply.

Here are some additional suggestions for finding an EV apprenticeship:

• Be proactive. Don't wait for apprenticeship programs to come to you. Start by researching programs in your area and contacting program sponsors to learn more.

• Be flexible. You may need to be willing to relocate for an apprenticeship program. You may also need to be willing to start at the bottom and work your way up.

• Be persistent. It may take some time to find an EV apprenticeship program that is a good fit for you. Don't give up.

Some of the benefits of an EV apprenticeship job include:

• Paid work experience: Apprentices are paid a salary while they learn and work. This can help cover the costs of living and education.

• Hands-on training: Apprentices learn from experienced EV technicians and have the opportunity to practice their skills in a real-world setting.

• Nationally recognized credentials: Upon completion of an EV apprenticeship program, apprentices earn a nationally recognized credential, such as an EV technician certificate or associate's degree. This credential can make them more competitive in the job market.

• Job security: The EV industry is growing rapidly, and EV technicians are in high demand. Apprentices who complete their programs can expect to have good job security.

EV apprenticeships are a great way to learn the skills you need to start a rewarding career in the fast-growing EV industry. If you are interested in an EV apprenticeship, I encourage you to start your search today.

Programs

Here is an example of an EV apprenticeship program:

Program: EV Technician Apprenticeship Program. Sponsor: National Electric Vehicle Infrastructure Training Program (NEVI). Length: 3 years. Requirements: High school diploma or equivalent, valid driver's license, and pass a background check.

• On-the-job training: Apprentices will work

under the supervision of experienced EV technicians at NEVI-approved training centers. They will learn how to diagnose and repair EV electrical systems, powertrains, and batteries. They will also learn how to safely maintain and inspect EVs.

• Classroom instruction: Apprentices will attend classroom instruction to learn the theoretical aspects of EV repair and maintenance. They will learn about the different types of EV motors and batteries, EV charging systems, and EV safety procedures.

• Credential: Upon completion of the program, apprentices will earn an EV Technician Certificate from the NEVI. This credential will make them more competitive in the job market and will qualify them for a variety of EV technician jobs.

This is just one example of an EV apprenticeship program. There are many other programs available, and they may vary in terms of length, requirements, and curriculum. I encourage you to research EV apprenticeship programs in your area to find one that is a good fit for you.

Tesla START

Tesla START is another example of an EV apprenticeship program. It is a paid, full-time training program that provides individuals with the skills and experience they need to become Tesla Service Technicians. The program lasts for 12 weeks and consists of on-the-job training at a Tesla Service Center, as well as classroom instruction.

During the on-the-job training, apprentices will learn how to diagnose and repair Tesla vehicles, including their electrical systems, powertrains, and batteries. They will also learn about Tesla's unique technologies, such as its Autopilot system. In the classroom, apprentices will learn about the theoretical aspects of EV repair and maintenance. They will also learn about Tesla's safety procedures and customer service standards.

Upon completion of the Tesla START program, apprentices will earn a Tesla Service Technician certification. This certification will make them qualified to work as Tesla Service Technicians at any Tesla Service Center in the world.

Some of the benefits of the Tesla START program include:
- Paid training
- Full-time employment at Tesla upon completion of the program
- Opportunity to learn from experienced Tesla

technicians

• Access to state-of-the-art Tesla equipment and facilities

• Nationally recognized certification

If you are interested in a career as a Tesla Service Technician, I encourage you to apply for the Tesla START program. It is a great way to learn the skills and experience you need to start a successful career in the EV industry.

How To Prepare

Following are some suggestions on how to prepare for an EV apprenticeship:

• Research EV apprenticeship programs. There are many different EV apprenticeship programs available, so it is important to research them and find one that is a good fit for you. Consider factors such as the length of the program, the requirements, the curriculum, and the location of the program.

• Gain experience in related fields. If you do not have any prior experience in the automotive or electrical fields, it is helpful to gain some experience before applying for an EV apprenticeship. You can do this by taking classes, volunteering, or working part-time in a related field.

• Develop your skills and knowledge. There are

a number of things you can do to develop your skills and knowledge in preparation for an EV apprenticeship. You can take online courses, read books and articles about EVs, or watch videos about EV repair and maintenance. You can also try to find a mentor who can help you learn more about EVs.

• Prepare your resume and cover letter. When you are ready to apply for an EV apprenticeship, be sure to prepare a strong resume and cover letter. Highlight your relevant skills and experience, and explain why you are interested in the apprenticeship program.

• Practice your interviewing skills. It is likely that you will need to interview for an EV apprenticeship program. Be sure to practice your interviewing skills so that you can make a good impression on the interviewer.

Here are some suggestions that may help you prepare for an EV apprenticeship:

• Network with people in the EV industry. Attend EV industry events, connect with people on LinkedIn, and reach out to people you know who may work in the EV industry. Networking can help you learn more about the industry and find out about EV apprenticeship opportunities.

• Be persistent. It may take some time to find

an EV apprenticeship program and get accepted. Don't give up. Keep applying for programs and networking with people in the industry.

Cost

The cost of an EV apprenticeship program varies depending on the program. Some programs are tuition-free, while others may charge a fee. It is important to research different programs and compare their costs before applying.

Factors that may affect the cost of an EV apprenticeship program include:

- The type of program: Some EV apprenticeship programs are offered by government agencies, while others are offered by private companies. Government-funded programs may be more likely to be tuition-free.
- The location of the program: EV apprenticeship programs in major metropolitan areas may be more expensive than programs in rural areas.
- The length of the program: Longer apprenticeship programs may be more expensive than shorter programs.
- The curriculum of the program: Apprenticeship programs that offer more comprehensive training may be more expensive than

programs that offer less comprehensive training.

In addition to tuition costs, there may be other out-of-pocket costs associated with an EV apprenticeship program, such as the cost of tools and books. It is important to factor in all of these costs when making your decision about which apprenticeship program to apply for.

BASIC TOOLS AND EQUIPMENT

There are some basic tools and equipment that are commonly used by EV technicians. These include:

- Basic hand tools: This includes screwdrivers, pliers, wrenches, and a hammer.
- Power tools: This includes a drill, impact driver, and saw.
- Electrical tools: This includes a multimeter, voltage tester, and insulated screwdrivers.
- EV-specific tools: This may include a battery pack service tool, high-voltage safety gear, and a diagnostic scanner.

In addition to tools and equipment, you may also need to purchase books and other training materials. Some apprenticeship programs may provide these materials for you, while others may require you to purchase them on your own.

If you are unsure about what tools and equipment you will need for your EV apprenticeship program, you should contact the program sponsor. They will be able to provide you with a list of the required tools and equipment.

Basic Hand Tools

The following are some of the most important basic hand tools that EV technicians need:

- Screwdrivers: EV technicians need a variety of screwdrivers to tighten and loosen screws of different sizes and types. Slotted, Phillips, and Torx screwdrivers are all essential for EV technicians.

- Pliers: Pliers are used to grip and bend wires, as well as to remove and install nuts and bolts. EV technicians need a variety of pliers, including lineman's pliers, channel lock pliers, and wire strippers.

- Wrenches: Wrenches are used to turn nuts and bolts. EV technicians need a variety of wrenches, including open-end wrenches, box-end wrenches, and adjustable wrenches.

- Sockets: Sockets are used with a ratchet or breaker bar to turn nuts and bolts. EV technicians need a variety of sockets, including metric and standard sockets, as well as deep and shallow sockets.

• Hammers: Hammers are used to drive nails and to loosen stuck nuts and bolts. EV technicians need a variety of hammers, including claw hammers and ball-peen hammers.

Power Tools

EV technicians need a variety of power tools to maintain and repair electric vehicles. The following are some of the most important power tools that EV technicians need:

• Drill: A drill is used to drill holes in a variety of materials, including metal, wood, and plastic. EV technicians use drills to install and remove screws and bolts, as well as to drill holes for wiring and other components.

• Impact driver: An impact driver is a type of power tool that is used to drive screws and bolts with high torque. EV technicians use impact drivers to tighten and loosen screws and bolts quickly and easily.

• Saw: A saw is used to cut a variety of materials, including metal, wood, and plastic. EV technicians use saws to cut body panels, wiring, and other components.

• Grinder: A grinder is a type of power tool that is used to remove material from a variety of surfaces.

EV technicians use grinders to remove rust, corrosion, and other debris from components.

• Soldering iron: A soldering iron is a type of power tool that is used to melt solder to create electrical connections. EV technicians use soldering irons to repair wiring and other electrical components.

It is important to note that EV technicians must use power tools safely. Power tools can be dangerous if not used properly. EV technicians should always wear appropriate safety gear when using power tools, such as safety glasses, hearing protection, and gloves.

EV technicians must use insulated tools when working on electric vehicles. This is because electric vehicles have high-voltage components that can cause serious injury or death if contacted. Insulated tools are designed to protect EV technicians from electrical shock.

Specialized Tools

Specialized tools are tools designed to help technicians work safely and efficiently on electric vehicles. Electric vehicles have high-voltage batteries and components that require special care and precautions when servicing or repairing them. Some of the specialized electrical and EV-specific tools that technicians use periodically include:

• Insulated tools: These are tools that have a protective coating or layer that prevents electric shocks or burns when working on live circuits. Insulated tools are tested and certified to withstand high voltages and currents. They are usually marked with the official 1000-volt rating symbol and the year of production. Some examples of insulated tools are pliers, ratchets, screwdrivers, sockets, and spanners.

• Multimeter: This is a device that measures various electrical properties, such as voltage, current, resistance, and continuity. A multimeter is essential for diagnosing and troubleshooting electrical problems in electric vehicles. It can also help to verify the proper functioning of sensors, switches, relays, and other components.

• Oscilloscope: This is a device that displays the waveform of an electrical signal over time. An oscilloscope can help to analyze the frequency, amplitude, shape, and phase of the signal. An oscilloscope can be useful for testing and monitoring the performance of inverters, converters, motors, and other high-voltage components in electric vehicles.

• Scan tool: This is a device that connects to the vehicle's onboard diagnostic system (OBD) and reads the trouble codes and data from various modules and sensors. A scan tool can help to identify and clear faults, perform tests, and access service information. A scan tool can also help to reprogram or update the software of some modules in electric vehicles.

• Personal protective equipment (PPE): This is the equipment that protects the technician from potential hazards when working on electric vehicles. PPE includes gloves, goggles, boots, clothing, and helmets that are rated for high-voltage exposure. PPE also includes insulated mats, blankets, and barriers that isolate and cover the high-voltage parts and components.

These are the important specialized tools that EV technicians need to work on electric vehicles safely and effectively.

High Quality Tools

Investing in high-quality tools is a wise decision for EV technicians. High-quality tools are safer, more durable, more accurate, more efficient, and more productive than low-quality tools. In addition, investing in high-quality tools can help EV technicians to stand out from their peers and attract more customers.

Here are some tips for choosing high-quality tools:

• Look for tools that are made from durable materials, such as chrome vanadium steel.

• Choose tools that have a comfortable grip and are easy to use.

• Select tools that are backed by a good warranty.

• Read reviews of different tools before you buy them.

• Compare prices of different tools before you buy them.

The amount of money that an EV technician expects to spend on essential tools and equipment can vary depending on a number of factors. However, as a general rule of thumb, EV technicians can expect to spend anywhere from $1,000 to $5,000 on essential tools and equipment.

Protective Gear

The following protective gear is recommended for EV technicians:

• Insulated gloves: Insulated gloves are essential for EV technicians to protect themselves from electrical shock. The gloves should be rated for the voltage of the electrical system they are working on.

• Insulated boots: Insulated boots protect EV

technicians from electrical shock if they accidentally step on a live wire. The boots should be rated for the voltage of the electrical system they are working on.

• Safety glasses: Safety glasses protect EV technicians from flying debris and eye injuries. They should be worn whenever working on electric vehicles.

• Hard hat: A hard hat protects EV technicians from head injuries. It should be worn whenever working in an area where there is a risk of falling objects.

• Face shield: A face shield protects EV technicians from flying debris and eye injuries. It should be worn whenever working on high-voltage components.

• Respirator: A respirator protects EV technicians from inhaling harmful fumes and dust. It should be worn when working on batteries, brakes, and other components that may produce harmful emissions.

• Earplugs: Earplugs protect EV technicians from noise-induced hearing loss. They should be worn when working in loud environments, such as repair shops and factories.

• Back brace: A back brace can help to prevent back injuries when lifting heavy objects. EV technicians should wear a back brace when lifting batteries and other heavy components.

In addition to the above, EV technicians may also want to wear other protective gear, such as:

• Knee pads: Knee pads protect EV technicians' knees from injury when working on the ground.

• Elbow pads: Elbow pads protect EV technicians' elbows from injury when working in cramped spaces.

• Safety vest: A safety vest makes EV technicians more visible to other workers and drivers.

It is important to note that all protective gear should be inspected regularly and replaced when necessary. EV technicians should also be trained on how to use and maintain their protective gear properly.

Training Manuals/Videos

EV technicians should invest in training manuals and videos. These resources can help them to stay up-to-date on the latest technologies and procedures for working on electric vehicles. Electric vehicles are a rapidly evolving technology, and new components and systems are being developed all the time. Training manuals and videos can help EV technicians to learn about these new technologies and how to work on them safely and effectively.

In addition to learning about new technologies, training manuals and videos can also help EV technicians to improve their skills. For example, a training video on how to diagnose a specific EV problem can help a technician to diagnose and repair that problem more quickly and accurately.

Training manuals and videos can also be a valuable resource for EV technicians who are new to the field. These resources can provide them with a foundation in the basics of EV technology and repair. Of course, training manuals and videos are not a substitute for hands-on experience. However, they can be a valuable supplement to hands-on training.

Investing in EV training resources is a wise decision because such resources can help EV technicians improve their skills and knowledge, which can lead to a more successful career.

Safety Standards
Safety is extremely important in an EV technician's job. Electric vehicles have high-voltage

components that can cause serious injury or death if not handled properly. EV technicians need to be aware of the hazards associated with working on electric vehicles and take steps to mitigate those hazards.

Here are some of the most important safety precautions that EV technicians need to take:

• Wear insulated gloves and boots whenever working on high-voltage components.

• Inspect all tools and equipment before using them to make sure that they are in good condition and insulated.

• Disconnect the high-voltage battery before working on any electrical components.

• Follow lockout/tagout procedures to prevent accidental energization of electrical systems.

• Be aware of the hazards associated with working on electric vehicles and take steps to mitigate those hazards.

EV technicians should also be familiar with the specific safety standards that are set by their employer and the manufacturers of the electric vehicles they work on. Failure to follow safety standards can have serious consequences. EV technicians who do not follow safety standards are at increased risk of electrical shock, burns, and other injuries. They may also cause damage to electric vehicles and other equipment.

In addition to protecting themselves, EV technicians who follow safety standards are also helping to protect their colleagues and customers.

Here are some additional tips for EV technicians to stay safe on the job:

• Get trained. EV technicians should complete comprehensive training on the safety procedures for working on electric vehicles. This training should cover topics such as electrical safety, lockout/tagout procedures, and hazard mitigation.

• Be prepared. EV technicians should have all of the necessary tools and equipment before starting any work on an electric vehicle. They should also make sure that they have a clear understanding of the work that needs to be done and the hazards involved.

• Be aware of your surroundings. EV technicians should be aware of their surroundings at all times when working on electric vehicles. They should be aware of the location of high-voltage components and other hazards.

• Take breaks. EV technicians should take breaks regularly to avoid fatigue. Fatigue can lead to mistakes and accidents.

• Report any concerns. EV technicians should report any concerns they have about safety to their supervisor immediately.

By following these guidelines, EV technicians can help to create a safer work environment for everyone.

Moving On...

In this chapter, we have learned about the educational and training requirements, apprenticeship programs, and essential tools of the EV technician's trade. In the next chapter, we will look at the fundamentals of electric vehicles.

3 EV FUNDAMENTALS

Understanding the fundamentals of electric vehicles is essential for EV technicians to work safely, accurately diagnose and repair problems, perform preventative maintenance, and prepare for the future of the automotive industry. In this chapter, we want to take a close look at:

- How EVs work
- Different types of EVs
- EV components and systems

Let us begin by examining how electric vehicles work.

HOW ELECTRIC VEHICLES WORK

It is important for EV technicians to understand

how electric vehicles work. EVs are vehicles that run on electricity, not on gasoline. They have a battery pack that stores the electricity and an electric motor that turns the wheels. EVs have several advantages over conventional cars, such as lower emissions, lower maintenance costs, and faster acceleration.

Here's a brief overview:

• EVs receive energy from a charging station and store the energy in their battery pack. The battery pack is usually located at the bottom of the vehicle between the wheels. The battery pack is made up of groups of lithium-ion cells, which are similar to the ones in your cell phone or laptop. The battery pack's capacity is measured in kilowatt-hours (kWh), which indicates how much energy it can hold and how far it can drive on a single charge. The larger the battery pack, the longer the range, but also the higher the cost and weight of the vehicle.

• The battery pack gives power to the electric motor, which moves the wheels. The electric motor is a device that converts electrical energy into mechanical energy. Unlike a gasoline engine, which has many moving parts and requires fuel and air to create combustion, an electric motor has fewer parts and does not need any fuel or air. This makes it more efficient, quieter, and more reliable than a gasoline engine. Some EVs have one electric motor, while others have two or more for better performance and traction.

• Many electrical parts work together in the background to make the EV run smoothly and safely. These include the power electronics, which control the flow of electricity from the battery to the motor; the thermal system, which regulates the temperature of the battery and other components; the regenerative braking system, which recovers some of the energy lost when braking and uses it to recharge the battery; and the onboard charger, which converts AC power from the grid to DC power for the battery.

EVs have high-voltage electrical systems, and if a technician is not trained on how to handle them safely, they could be putting themselves in danger. High voltage can lead to electric shock, fire, and other hazardous situations. In addition, EVs are complex machines, and technicians need to understand how they work in order to diagnose and repair problems effectively. Without proper training, technicians may struggle to fix EVs, leading to longer repair times and higher costs for customers.

EV technicians who understand the basics of EV

technology are better equipped to safely and effectively repair and maintain EVs. This is important for the safety of the technician, the customer, and the vehicle itself. It is also important for EV technicians to understand the latest EV trends and technologies. This will help them to stay ahead of the curve and provide the best possible service to their customers.

Differences Between EVs and Conventional Vehicles

EV technicians must be aware of the differences between electric vehicles and conventional or gas-powered vehicles. Some of the differences between EVs and gas-powered vehicles including:

• Fuel source: Electric vehicles use electricity stored in a battery pack to power an electric motor, while gas-powered vehicles use gasoline burned in an internal combustion engine to power a mechanical drivetrain. This means that electric vehicles do not produce any tailpipe emissions, while gas-powered vehicles emit carbon dioxide and other pollutants into the air. Electric vehicles can be charged from various sources of electricity, such as renewable energy, nuclear power, or fossil fuels, while gas-powered vehicles rely on a limited supply of oil that is often imported from other countries.

- Fuel economy: Electric vehicles are more efficient than gas-powered vehicles, as they convert more of the energy from their fuel source into motion. According to the U.S. Department of Energy, electric vehicles can travel about 100 miles on 27 to 40 kWh of electricity, while gas-powered vehicles can travel about 100 miles on 3 to 4 gallons of gasoline. This means that electric vehicles can save money on fuel costs, as electricity is generally cheaper than gasoline per unit of energy. However, the actual cost savings depend on the local price of electricity and gasoline, as well as the driving habits and conditions of the driver.

- Maintenance: Electric vehicles have fewer moving parts than gas-powered vehicles, which means they require less maintenance and repairs. Electric vehicles do not need oil changes, spark plugs, air filters, or other components that are common in gas-powered vehicles. The main maintenance item for electric vehicles is the battery pack, which may degrade over time and lose some of its capacity and range. However, most electric vehicle manufacturers offer warranties for their battery packs that last for several years or miles.

- Performance: Electric vehicles have several advantages over gas-powered vehicles when it comes to performance. Electric motors can deliver instant torque and acceleration, which makes them faster and more responsive than gas engines. Electric motors can also operate at a wider range of speeds and power levels, which eliminates the need for a transmission and improves the efficiency and smoothness of the vehicle. Electric vehicles also have a lower center of gravity and better weight distribution than gas-powered vehicles, which improves their handling and stability.

• Range: One of the main drawbacks of electric vehicles is their limited range compared to gas-powered vehicles. The range of an electric vehicle depends on the size and capacity of its battery pack, as well as the driving conditions and habits of the driver. The average range of an electric vehicle in the U.S. is about 250 miles, while the average range of a gas-powered vehicle is about 400 miles. However, some electric vehicles can achieve much higher ranges, such as the Tesla Model S Long Range Plus, which can travel up to 405 miles on a single charge. The range anxiety of electric vehicle drivers can be alleviated by the availability and accessibility of charging stations, which are becoming more widespread and faster in recent years.

Advantages of EVs
EVs have several advantages over their gas-

powered counterparts. These advantages can be described as:

- Cleaner environment: Electric vehicles have no tailpipe emissions, which means they do not contribute to local air pollution and greenhouse gas emissions that can harm human health and the environment. Electric vehicles can also use renewable sources of electricity, such as solar or wind power, to further reduce their environmental impact.

- Lower fuel costs: Electric vehicles are cheaper to run than gasoline or diesel vehicles, as electricity is generally less expensive than fossil fuels per unit of energy. Electric vehicles also have higher efficiency, as they convert more of the energy from their fuel source into motion. According to the U.S. Department of Energy, electric vehicles can travel about 100 miles on 27 to 40 kWh of electricity, while gas-powered vehicles can travel about 100 miles on 3 to 4 gallons of gasoline.

- Lower maintenance costs: Electric vehicles have fewer moving parts and do not require oil changes, spark plugs, air filters, or other components that are common in gas-powered vehicles. This means they need less frequent servicing and repairs, which can save money and time for owners. The main maintenance item for electric vehicles is the battery pack, which may degrade over time and lose some of its capacity and range. However, most electric vehicle manufacturers offer warranties for their battery packs that last for several years or miles.

• Better driving experience: Electric vehicles offer a smooth and quiet ride, as they have no gears and produce minimal noise. Electric motors also deliver instant torque and acceleration, which makes them faster and more responsive than gas engines. Electric vehicles also have a lower center of gravity and better weight distribution than gas-powered vehicles, which improves their handling and stability.

• Various incentives and benefits: Electric vehicle owners can enjoy various incentives and benefits from the government and other organizations, such as tax credits, rebates, grants, discounts, free parking, solo access to carpool lanes, and more. These incentives and benefits can lower the initial purchase price and the operating costs of electric vehicles, as well as encourage more people to switch to cleaner transportation options.

Let us turn our attention to the different types of electric vehicles.

DIFFERENT TYPES OF EVs

It is important for EV technicians to understand

the different types of EVs. There are four main types of EVs on the market. They can be described as:

• Battery electric vehicles (BEVs): These are vehicles that run on electricity only and do not have any gasoline engine or fuel tank. They have a large battery pack that stores the electricity and can be recharged from an external source, such as a wall outlet or a charging station. BEVs have zero tailpipe emissions and can offer a long driving range, depending on the size and capacity of the battery. Some examples of BEVs are the Tesla Model 3, the Chevrolet Bolt, and the Nissan Leaf.

• Plug-in hybrid electric vehicles (PHEVs): These are vehicles that have both an electric motor and a gasoline engine. They have a smaller battery pack than BEVs, but they can also be recharged from an external source. PHEVs can drive on electricity alone for a limited distance, usually 20 to 50 miles, before switching to the gasoline engine for longer trips. PHEVs have lower emissions and fuel consumption than conventional vehicles, especially for short trips. Some examples of PHEVs are the Toyota Prius Prime, the Ford Escape Plug-in Hybrid, and the Mitsubishi Outlander PHEV.

• Hybrid electric vehicles (HEVs): These are vehicles that have both an electric motor and a gasoline engine, but they cannot be recharged from an external source. They have a small battery pack that is recharged by the gasoline engine or by regenerative braking, which recovers some of the energy lost when slowing down or stopping. HEVs use the electric motor to assist the gasoline engine, which improves fuel efficiency and reduces emissions. HEVs cannot drive on electricity alone, except for very short distances and low speeds. Some examples of HEVs are the Toyota Prius, the Honda Insight, and the Hyundai Ioniq Hybrid.

• Fuel cell electric vehicles (FCEVs): These are vehicles that use hydrogen gas as fuel to generate electricity in a device called a fuel cell. The electricity then powers an electric motor that drives the wheels. FCEVs have zero tailpipe emissions, except for water vapor, and can offer a long driving range, similar to gasoline vehicles. However, FCEVs are not widely available and require special hydrogen refueling stations, which are scarce and expensive. Some examples of FCEVs are the Toyota Mirai, the Honda Clarity Fuel Cell, and the Hyundai Nexo.

Maintenance

In general, electric vehicles require less and less frequent maintenance than conventional vehicles, as they have fewer moving parts and fluids. However, they still need some regular servicing and checks to ensure their safety, performance, and warranty. Some of the common maintenance items for electric car servicing are:

• Air filters: These are used to filter the air that enters the cabin and the battery cooling system. They need to be replaced periodically, depending on the driving conditions and the manufacturer's recommendations.

• Brake fluid: This is a hydraulic fluid that transfers the braking force from the pedal to the wheels. It needs to be checked and changed every two years or so, as it can absorb moisture and degrade over time.

• Tire rotation, alignment, replacement, and balance: These are essential for any car, as tires affect the handling, traction, and efficiency of the vehicle. They need to be rotated every 5,000 to 10,000 miles, aligned every year or two, replaced when the tread depth is below 2/32 inches, and balanced when there is vibration or uneven wear.

• Brake calipers: These are the metal clamps that squeeze the brake pads against the rotors to slow down the car. They need to be cleaned and lubricated occasionally, as they can get rusty or sticky due to low usage in electric cars that rely more on regenerative braking.

• Battery: This is the heart of an electric car, as

it stores and provides the electrical energy for propulsion. It needs to be monitored for its health, capacity, and temperature, as these can affect its performance and lifespan. Most electric car batteries are designed to last for at least eight years or 100,000 miles, and come with a warranty that covers any significant degradation or failure.

• Coolant: This is a liquid that circulates through the battery and the electric motor to prevent them from overheating. It needs to be checked and topped up every few years, or according to the manufacturer's specifications.

• Electric motor: This is the device that converts electrical energy into mechanical energy to drive the wheels. It needs to be inspected for any signs of wear or damage, such as loose connections, corrosion, or abnormal noises.

• Power electronics: These are the components that control and regulate the flow of electricity between the battery, the motor, and the charger. They include inverters, converters, relays, fuses, and sensors. They need to be checked for any faults or malfunctions, such as overheating, short circuits, or software glitches.

These are some of the common maintenance items for electric vehicles. However, different models may have different requirements and schedules, so it is best to check the vehicle's owner's manual and dealer specifications.

EV COMPONENTS AND SYSTEMS

EVs have several components and systems that work together to make them run smoothly and efficiently. Here are some of the main components and systems of EVs:

• Traction battery pack: This is the component that stores the electricity for the vehicle. It is usually located at the bottom of the vehicle between the wheels. The battery pack is made up of groups of lithium-ion cells, which are similar to the ones in your cell phone or laptop. The battery pack's capacity is measured in kilowatt-hours (kWh), which indicates how much energy it can hold and how far it can drive on a single charge. The larger the battery pack, the longer the range, but also the higher the cost and weight of the vehicle.

• DC-DC converter: This is the device that converts higher-voltage DC power from the traction battery pack to lower-voltage DC power needed to run vehicle accessories and recharge the auxiliary battery. The auxiliary battery is a smaller battery that provides electricity to power vehicle accessories, such as lights, radio, and air conditioning.

• Electric motor: This is the device that converts electrical energy into mechanical energy. It uses power from the traction battery pack to turn the wheels and move the vehicle. Unlike a gasoline engine, which has many moving parts and requires fuel and air to create combustion, an electric motor has fewer parts and does not need any fuel or air. This makes it more efficient, quieter, and more reliable than a gasoline engine. Some EVs have one electric motor, while others have two or more for better performance and traction.

• Power inverter: This is the device that converts DC power from the batteries to AC power for the electric motor. It also controls the speed and torque of the electric motor by varying the frequency and voltage of the AC power.

• Charge port: This is the component that allows the vehicle to connect to an external power supply, such as a wall outlet or a charging station, in order to charge the traction battery pack. The charge port can have different shapes and sizes depending on the type and standard of charging used by the vehicle.

• Onboard charger: This is the device that takes the incoming AC electricity supplied via the charge port and converts it to DC power for charging the traction battery. It also communicates with the charging equipment and monitors battery characteristics such as voltage, current, temperature, and state of charge while charging the pack.

- Controller: This is the unit that manages the flow of electrical energy delivered by the traction battery, controlling the speed of the electric motor and the torque it produces. It also regulates other functions such as regenerative braking, which recovers some of the energy lost when braking and uses it to recharge the battery.

- Thermal system: This is the system that maintains a proper operating temperature range of the engine, electric motor, power electronics, and other components. It uses coolant fluids, fans, pumps, radiators, and heaters to keep them from overheating or freezing.

In addition to these main components, EVs also have a number of important systems, including:

- Regenerative braking system: The regenerative braking system converts the kinetic energy of the EV into electricity, which is then stored in the battery pack. This helps to extend the range of the EV on a single charge.

- Infotainment system: The infotainment system provides the driver and passengers with access to music, navigation, and other entertainment features.

• Safety systems: EVs are equipped with a variety of safety systems, such as airbags, anti-lock brakes, and traction control.

• Connectivity: EVs are increasingly being equipped with connectivity features, such as Bluetooth, Wi-Fi, and cellular connectivity. This allows the driver to connect their smartphone to the EV and access a variety of features, such as remote start and climate control.

These are some of the important components and systems of an electric vehicle. As EV technology continues to develop, we can expect to see even more innovative and efficient designs in the future.

Moving On…

In this chapter, we have looked at the fundamentals of EVs: How they operate, the different types of EVs and the important components and systems of EVs. In the next chapter, we will explore EV safety as it relates to the job.

4 EV SAFETY

Safety is an important consideration for EV technicians, because working on electric vehicles involves different hazards and risks than working on conventional vehicles. In this chapter, we will consider common safety risks and the procedures to follow when servicing EVs. Specifically, we want to look at:
- High-voltage safety procedures
- Working with EV batteries
- Servicing EV motors and drives

Let's begin by looking at high voltage safety procedures.

HIGH VOLTAGE SAFETY PROCEDURES

EVs are very safe vehicles. However, it is important to be aware of the potential safety risks associated with high voltage systems. By taking appropriate precautions, you can help to reduce the risk of injury or harm. Some common high voltage hazards associated with EVs include:

• Electric shock: Even small currents from high voltage systems can cause serious injury or death. This can occur if a person comes into contact with exposed high voltage wires or components.

• Arc flash: An arc flash is a sudden release of intense heat and light that can occur when high voltage circuits are interrupted. Arc flashes can cause severe burns and eye damage. This can occur if a person is working on a high voltage system and accidentally creates a short circuit.

• Thermal runaway: Thermal runaway is a chain reaction that can occur in lithium-ion batteries, leading to a fire or explosion. This can occur if a battery is damaged or overheated.

• Electromagnetic fields (EMFs): EMFs are invisible fields of energy that can be produced by high voltage systems. Long-term exposure to EMFs has been linked to a number of health problems, such as cancer. However, the level of EMF exposure from EVs is generally considered to be low.

Other potential hazards associated with working on EVs can include:

• Accidental activation of high voltage systems: High voltage systems in EVs can be accidentally activated if the vehicle is not properly de-energized. This can occur if a person is working on the vehicle and accidentally turns on the power.

• Improper use of tools and equipment: Using the wrong tools or equipment can create a risk of electric shock or arc flash. It is important to use insulated tools and equipment that are designed for working on high voltage systems.

• Failure to follow safety procedures: Not following manufacturer's safety procedures can increase the risk of injury or harm. It is important to read and follow all safety instructions before working on an EV.

By being aware of the potential hazards associated with high voltage systems, you can help to reduce the risk of harming yourself and others.

High Voltage Safety

Safety, especially high-voltage safety, is very important for someone who works with or around EVs. EVs have high-voltage components and systems that can pose serious hazards if not handled properly. Some of the fundamentals of high voltage safety for EV technicians are:

• Understanding the types and characteristics of EVs: EVs as you know can be classified into different types, such as hybrid electric vehicles (HEVs), plug-in hybrid electric vehicles (PHEVs), battery electric vehicles (BEVs), and fuel cell electric vehicles (FCEVs). Each type of EV has different characteristics, such as powertrain configuration, energy storage system, charging system, and high-voltage components. EV technicians should be familiar with the specific features and functions of each type of EV and how they affect the safety procedures and practices.

• Identifying and locating high-voltage components: High-voltage components are the parts of an EV that operate at voltages above 60 volts DC or 30 volts AC. They are usually colored orange or blue to indicate their potential danger. Some examples of high-voltage components are batteries, inverters, converters, motors, generators, cables, connectors, fuses, relays, switches, and sensors. EV technicians should be able to identify and locate the high-voltage components on any EV model and know their functions and specifications.

• Using proper personal protective equipment (PPE): PPE is a vital part of high-voltage safety. It includes heavy, rubber, Class 0 rated gloves, face shield, rubber apron, insulated tools, and non-conductive footwear. PPE should be inspected regularly for any damage or defects and replaced if necessary. PPE should be worn whenever working on or near high-voltage components or systems.

• Following the high-voltage disconnecting procedure: Before working on or near any high-voltage components or systems, the high-voltage system should be de-energized and isolated from the rest of the vehicle. This involves turning off the ignition, setting up a barrier, placing a warning sign, removing the negative terminal of the 12V battery, locating the service disconnect plug or switch, and verifying the absence of voltage. The service disconnect plug or switch is a device that allows the separation of the high-voltage system from the battery pack. It is usually located under the hood, in the trunk, or under the rear seat. The absence of voltage can be verified by using a digital multimeter or a non-contact voltage tester.

• Avoiding contact with high-voltage cables: High-voltage cables are usually colored orange or blue to indicate their potential danger. They should not be touched, cut, spliced, or modified unless the high-voltage system has been disconnected. They should also be routed away from any heat sources or sharp edges. If a high-voltage cable is damaged or exposed, it should be repaired or replaced by a qualified technician.

• Being aware of electromagnetic fields (EMFs): High-voltage electricity generates EMFs that can affect the health and safety of workers and others in the vicinity. EMFs can interfere with the functioning of medical devices such as pacemakers and implantable defibrillators. Workers with such devices should consult their doctors before working on or near high-voltage vehicles. They should also avoid wearing any metal objects or jewelry that may conduct electricity.

• Receiving proper training and certification: Working with high-voltage vehicles requires specialized knowledge and skills that can only be acquired through proper training and certification. Workers should receive high-voltage electrical training from reputable sources such as DEKRA Training, ASE | Automotive Service Excellence, SAE International, Weber State University, or TÜV SÜD. They should also keep up to date with the latest developments and technologies in the EV industry.

Being aware of the fundamentals of high voltage safety enables technicians to handle high-voltage electricity in electric vehicles without causing harm to themselves or others.

High Voltage Safety Training

High voltage safety training is essential for EV technicians to protect themselves and others from the hazards associated with high voltage systems. By completing comprehensive high voltage safety training, EV technicians can help to ensure their safety and the safety of others.

There are different levels of training and certification available for EV technicians, depending on their roles and responsibilities. One of the sources that provides high-voltage safety training for EV technicians is DEKRA Training. They offer online, face-to-face, and customized courses that cover topics such as identifying and locating high-voltage components, working safely near high-voltage components, de-energizing procedures, safety equipment and personal protective equipment, and first aid and emergency procedures. They also have access to a database of manufacturer information for all EVs.

Another source is ASE (Automotive Service Excellence), which offers EV High-Voltage Electrical

Safety certifications for different levels of EV professionals. The Level 1 certification is for anyone who may encounter an EV in the workplace, such as sales, service, repair, or support personnel. The Level 2 certification is for service professionals, technicians, or specialists who have received high-voltage electrical training and demonstrated skills and knowledge related to the construction, operation, and repair of electrically powered high-voltage vehicles. They also provide Electrical Safety Standards that serve as a guide for the industry.

Other sources that offer high-voltage safety training for EV technicians are SAE International, Weber State University, and FutureTech. They have various courses and programs that cover the fundamentals of high voltage safety and PPE. They also provide practical exercises and hands-on experience with high-voltage vehicles and systems.

A high voltage safety training should cover a range of topics, including:

• Overview of EV technology: This should include the different types of EVs, their components, and how they work.

• The risks and hazards associated with high voltage systems: This should include the different types of electric shock, the effects of electric shock on the body, and how to identify and avoid hazards.

•   Safety procedures for working with high voltage systems: This should include lockout/tagout procedures, grounding procedures, and testing procedures.

•   Use and maintenance of personal protective equipment (PPE): This should include the different types of PPE used for working with high voltage systems, how to properly use and maintain PPE, and how to inspect PPE for damage.

•   Emergency procedures: This should include first aid procedures for electric shock and other injuries, as well as fire suppression procedures.

In addition to these general topics, high voltage safety training should also cover specific topics related to the EVs that technicians will be working on. This may include information on the location of high voltage components, specific lockout/tagout procedures, and specific testing procedures.

Any high voltage safety training should be conducted by a qualified instructor and should be hands-on in nature. Technicians should have the opportunity to practice the safety procedures that they have learned in a safe environment.

WORKING WITH EV BATTERIES

EV batteries are devices that store and convert chemical energy into electricity. They power the electric motor or motors that drive the vehicle. EV batteries are made of many electrochemical cells that have two electrodes and an electrolyte. The electrodes are usually made of metal oxides and graphite, and the electrolyte is a liquid solution that contains lithium ions. When the battery is charged, the lithium ions move from the positive electrode to the negative electrode through the electrolyte, and the electrons flow through an external circuit. When the battery is discharged, the process reverses and the electrons power the motor.

Types

There are four main types of EV batteries that are commonly used today:

• Lithium-ion batteries: These are the most popular type of EV batteries and are also found in consumer electronic devices like smartphones, laptops, and cameras. Lithium-ion batteries have high energy density, which means they can store a lot of energy in a small space. They also have high power density, which means they can deliver a lot of power in a short time. They have long lifespan, high efficiency, and low self-discharge rate. However, they are also expensive, sensitive to temperature, and prone to degradation over time.

• Nickel-metal hydride batteries: These are another type of EV batteries that are mainly used in hybrid electric vehicles (HEVs), such as the Toyota Prius. Nickel-metal hydride batteries have lower energy density and power density than lithium-ion batteries, but they are cheaper, more durable, and more environmentally friendly. They also have good performance in cold weather and high self-discharge rate.

• Lead-acid batteries: These are the oldest type of EV batteries and are still used in some low-cost and low-performance EVs. Lead-acid batteries have very low energy density and power density, which means they are heavy and bulky. They also have short lifespan, low efficiency, and high maintenance cost. However, they are very cheap, easy to recycle, and widely available.

• Ultracapacitor batteries: These are a new type of EV batteries that are not actually batteries, but devices that store electrical energy in an electric field. Ultracapacitor batteries have very high power density, which means they can charge and discharge very quickly. They also have long lifespan, high efficiency, and low self-discharge rate. However, they have very low energy density, which means they can store very little energy. They are also very expensive and require complex management systems.

Safety Procedures

Here are some of the fundamentals for working safely with EV batteries:

• Understanding the types and characteristics of EV batteries: EV batteries are mostly lithium-ion batteries, which have high energy density, high voltage, and long lifespan. They are composed of many electrochemical cells that store and release electricity through the movement of lithium ions and electrons. There are different types of lithium-ion batteries, such as NMC, LFP, NCA, and LTO, which have different compositions, performances, and applications. EV batteries also have battery management systems (BMS) that monitor and control the battery's state of charge, temperature, voltage, current, and health.

• Identifying and locating high-voltage components: High-voltage components are the parts of an EV that operate at voltages above 60 volts DC or 30 volts AC. They are usually colored orange or blue to indicate their potential danger. Some examples of high-voltage components are batteries, inverters, converters, motors, generators, cables, connectors, fuses, relays, switches, and sensors. You should be able to identify and locate the high-voltage components on any EV model and know their functions and specifications.

• Using proper personal protective equipment (PPE): PPE is a vital part of high-voltage safety. It includes heavy, rubber, Class 0 rated gloves, face shield, rubber apron, insulated tools, and non-conductive footwear. PPE should be inspected regularly for any damage or defects and replaced if necessary. PPE should be worn whenever working on or near high-voltage components or systems.

• Following the high-voltage disconnecting procedure: Before working on or near any high-voltage components or systems, the high-voltage system should be de-energized and isolated from the rest of the vehicle. This involves turning off the ignition, setting up a barrier, placing a warning sign, removing the negative terminal of the 12V battery, locating the service disconnect plug or switch, and verifying the absence of voltage. The service disconnect plug or switch is a device that allows the separation of the high-voltage system from the battery pack. It is usually located under the hood, in the trunk, or under the rear seat. The absence of voltage can be verified by using a digital multimeter or a non-contact voltage tester.

• Avoiding contact with high-voltage cables: High-voltage cables are usually colored orange or blue to indicate their potential danger. They should not be touched, cut, spliced, or modified unless the high-voltage system has been disconnected. They should also be routed away from any heat sources or sharp edges. If a high-voltage cable is damaged or exposed, it should be repaired or replaced by a qualified technician.

• Being aware of electromagnetic fields (EMFs): High-voltage electricity generates EMFs that can affect the health and safety of workers and others in the vicinity. EMFs can interfere with the functioning of medical devices such as pacemakers and implantable defibrillators. Workers with such devices should consult their doctors before working on or near high-voltage vehicles. They should also avoid wearing any metal objects or jewelry that may conduct electricity.

• Receiving proper training and certification: Working with EV batteries requires specialized knowledge and skills that can only be acquired through proper training and certification.

SERVICING EV MOTORS AND DRIVES

Servicing EV motors and drives is an important aspect of maintaining electric vehicles. Electric motors and drives are the components that convert electrical energy into mechanical energy, and they need to be kept in good condition to ensure optimal performance and efficiency. Here are some things you need to know about servicing EV motors and drives:

- EV motors and drives are generally more reliable and durable than internal combustion engines, but they still require regular inspection and cleaning to prevent overheating, corrosion, and damage.

- EV motors and drives may need lubrication, alignment, balancing, or replacement of worn parts depending on the type and usage of the vehicle. Some EVs have a gearbox or transmission that also needs servicing according to the manufacturer's recommendations.

- EV motors and drives are sensitive to extreme temperatures, moisture, dust, and debris, so they should be protected from these environmental factors as much as possible. You should avoid parking an EV in direct sunlight, high humidity, or dusty areas for long periods of time.

- EV motors and drives are connected to the battery pack, which is the most expensive and critical component of an EV. The battery pack needs to be monitored for its state of charge, state of health, and temperature, and it should be charged and discharged properly to extend its lifespan. You should avoid fully charging or depleting the battery, and use fast chargers sparingly.

• EV motors and drives should be serviced by either a manufacturer-approved dealership or an independent garage that has the necessary equipment and expertise to handle EVs.

Common Problems

Some common problems associated with EV motors and drives are:

• Overheating: EV motors and drives generate heat during operation, which can affect their efficiency and performance. Overheating can also damage the motor windings, bearings, and other components. To prevent overheating, EV motors and drives need adequate cooling systems, such as air, water, or oil cooling.

• Corrosion: EV motors and drives are exposed to moisture, dust, and debris, which can cause corrosion and rust on the metal parts. Corrosion can reduce the conductivity and durability of the motor and drive components, leading to increased resistance and power loss. To prevent corrosion, EV motors and drives need proper protection and insulation from the environment.

• Torque ripple: EV motors and drives produce torque that varies with the rotational position of the rotor. This variation, known as torque ripple, can cause vibration, noise, and wear on the motor and drive components. Torque ripple can also affect the smoothness and accuracy of the vehicle's acceleration and deceleration. To reduce torque ripple, EV motors and drives need advanced control algorithms, such as field-oriented control or direct torque control.

• Torsion: EV motors and drives are connected to the driveline, which transfers the torque to the wheels. The driveline consists of various components, such as shafts, couplings, gears, and differentials. These components can introduce torsion, or twisting force, on the motor and drive shafts. Torsion can cause stress, fatigue, and failure on the motor and drive components. To minimize torsion, EV motors and drives need proper alignment, balancing, and damping of the driveline components.

The frequency of servicing motors and drives depends on the make, model, mileage, and condition of the vehicle. However, some general guidelines are:

- EV motors and drives should be serviced at least once a year or every 10,000 to 20,000 miles, whichever comes first.
- EV motors and drives may need more frequent servicing if they are exposed to extreme temperatures, moisture, dust, or debris.
- EV motors and drives should be serviced by a qualified technician.

Servicing EV motors and drives can help extend their lifespan, improve their performance and efficiency, and prevent costly repairs.

Moving On….

In this chapter, we have looked at some common safety hazards and the proper procedures to follow when servicing EV high-voltage components, batteries, motors and drives. In the following chapter, we will study EV maintenance and repair.

5 EV MAINTENANCE AND REPAIR

Electric vehicles are becoming more popular and affordable, but they also require special care and attention. EV maintenance and repair is different from conventional vehicles, and it is important to know the basics of how to keep EVs running smoothly and safely.

In this chapter, we will study EV maintenance and repair. We will be discussing:
- Routine maintenance tasks
- Troubleshooting common EV problems
- Battery pack replacement
- Motor and drive repair

Let's begin by looking at some routine maintenance tasks for electric vehicles.

ROUTINE MAINTENANCE TASKS

EVs generally require less maintenance than conventional vehicles, but they still need periodic attention. Here are some of the common routine maintenance tasks for EVs:

• Battery testing: The battery is the most important and expensive component of an EV, and it needs to be monitored for its state of charge, state of health, and temperature. Battery testing can help you ensure that your battery is charging properly and efficiently, and that it is not degrading too fast. You can use a battery management system or a diagnostic tool to check your battery's status and performance.

• Tire rotation: EVs have more weight on their tires due to the heavy battery pack, and they also have more torque that can cause uneven wear on the tires. Tire rotation can help you extend the lifespan of your tires and improve your vehicle's handling and safety. You should rotate your tires every 5,000 to 10,000 miles, or according to your manufacturer's recommendations.

• Brake fluid replacement: EVs use regenerative braking, which reduces the use of the conventional friction brakes. However, the brake fluid still needs to be replaced periodically to prevent corrosion and contamination in the brake system. You should replace your brake fluid every two years or 20,000 miles, or according to your manufacturer's recommendations.

• Cabin air filter replacement: The cabin air filter cleans the air that enters the vehicle's interior, and it can get clogged with dust, pollen, and other particles over time. A dirty cabin air filter can affect the quality of the air you breathe and the performance of the air conditioning system. You should replace your cabin air filter every 15,000 to 30,000 miles, or according to your manufacturer's recommendations.

• Battery thermal management coolant flush: EVs have a cooling system that regulates the temperature of the battery pack and other components. The cooling system uses a special coolant that circulates through pipes and radiators. The coolant can degrade over time and lose its effectiveness, which can affect the battery's performance and lifespan. You should flush and replace your battery thermal management coolant every four years or 50,000 miles, or according to your manufacturer's recommendations.

EVs share many common maintenance items with conventional vehicles, such as tires, brakes, suspension, steering, lights, wipers, and cabin filters. These items need to be checked and replaced periodically to ensure optimal performance and safety. EVs also have some unique features and systems that require special care, such as regenerative braking, high-voltage wiring, plug-in charging, and software updates. These features and systems require troubleshooting or repair when they malfunction or fail.

EVs should be serviced by qualified technicians at a manufacturer-approved dealership or an independent repair shop that has the necessary equipment and expertise to handle EV maintenance and repairs. Servicing an EV may vary depending on the make, model, mileage, and condition of the vehicle.

Battery Maintenance

The health of an electric vehicle's battery is an important factor that affects its performance, range, and lifespan. There are different ways to check the battery health of an electric vehicle, depending on the make and model of the car. Here are some common methods that you can use:

• Check the estimated range on the dashboard. This is the simplest way to get an idea of how much charge your battery can hold and how far you can drive on a full charge. However, this method is not very accurate, as the range can vary depending on driving conditions, weather, and other factors. Also, some electric vehicles may not display the range on the dashboard.

• Check the state of charge (SOC) of the battery. This is the percentage of charge left in the battery at any given time. You can usually see this on the dashboard or the infotainment screen of your electric vehicle. A healthy battery should have a high SOC, meaning it can store more energy. A low SOC indicates that the battery is losing capacity and may need to be replaced soon.

• Check the voltage and current of the battery. This is a more technical way to measure the health of the battery, as it requires using a multimeter or a diagnostic tool to connect to the battery terminals. The voltage is the electrical potential of the battery, and the current is the rate of flow of electricity in and out of the battery. A healthy battery should have a voltage of 12.6 volts or more, and a current flow of 3-5 amps. If the voltage or current is too low or too high, it may indicate a problem with the battery or the charging system.

Some common problems with electric vehicle

batteries include:

• Faulty or damaged separator. This is a thin layer that separates the positive and negative electrodes of the battery and prevents them from short-circuiting. If the separator is defective or worn out, it can cause the battery to overheat, catch fire, or explode.

• Temperature sensitivity. The performance and lifespan of the battery depend on the ambient temperature and the temperature of the battery itself. Extreme heat or cold can reduce the battery capacity and range, damage the internal components, or trigger safety mechanisms that limit the charging or discharging rate.

• Premature capacity loss. This is the gradual decline of the battery's ability to store and deliver energy over time and use. All batteries lose some capacity with age, but some factors can accelerate this process, such as overcharging, deep discharging, high current, or poor maintenance.

• In-car electronics, noises and leaks, power equipment, climate system, body hardware, drive system, and paint and trim. These are some of the problem areas that affect the reliability of electric vehicles, according to a Consumer Reports survey. Some of these issues may be related to the battery or the charging system, while others may be due to the design or quality of the vehicle.

There are different ways to care for an EV battery, depending on the type, model, and usage of the vehicle. Some general points to keep in mind are:

• Fully charge and balance the battery. This means charging the battery to 100 percent and letting it stay there for a few hours. This helps to equalize the voltage and capacity of the individual cells in the battery pack and prevent degradation.

• Extended storage. Someone who is not going to use his car for a long time should store it with a moderate charge level, around 50 percent. This prevents the battery from losing too much charge or getting overcharged by a plugged-in charger.

• Avoid extreme temperature conditions. High or low temperatures can affect the battery's performance and lifespan. An EV should be parked in a shaded or covered area, avoid exposing it to direct sunlight or freezing weather, and use the climate control system to keep the battery at an optimal temperature.

• Avoid deep discharge. Deep discharging means draining the battery to a very low level, below 10 percent. This can damage the battery and reduce its capacity. Try to keep the battery between 20 and 80 percent charged for daily use.

• Don't leave the battery at a 100 percent state of charge for too long. This can harm the battery and cause it to lose capacity over time. An EV battery should only be charged to 100 percent when the maximum range is needed and use it as soon as possible. Some cars have settings to limit the maximum charge level to 85 or 90 percent for regular use.

Following these suggestions can help maintain an EV battery and extend its life.

Brake Maintenance

Regenerative braking is a system that allows an EV to recover some of the kinetic energy that would otherwise be wasted as heat when the vehicle slows down or stops. By using an electric motor or generator to convert this kinetic energy into electrical energy, the regenerative braking system can recharge the battery and extend the driving range of the EV.

Regenerative braking systems are becoming more common in electric and hybrid vehicles, but they are also available in a few gasoline-powered vehicles. So what exactly is regenerative braking system maintenance? How does it work? And are there any smart tips for maintenance of EV brakes? Here are some of the main points that you should know:

• Regenerative braking systems are usually controlled by a computer or a controller that determines the optimal amount of regenerative braking and friction braking to apply in different situations. Therefore, it is important to have a regular battery inspection and any software updates that may be available, completed by a certified service technician.

• Regenerative braking systems often have a user interface or a display that shows the driver the amount of energy recovered and the state of charge of the battery. You should check this information periodically and make sure that the battery is not overcharged or undercharged, as this can affect the performance and lifespan of the battery.

• Regenerative braking systems may have different modes or settings that allow the driver to adjust the level of regencrative braking, such as normal, low, or high. You should use the mode that suits your driving style and terrain, and avoid switching modes frequently, as this can cause stress on the battery and the electric motor.

• Regenerative braking systems can reduce the wear and tear on the conventional friction brakes, which can lower the maintenance costs and emissions of the EV. However, this does not mean that you can neglect the friction brakes completely. You should still perform periodic maintenance checks on the entire braking system, such as cleaning the brake pads, rotors, calipers, and fluid, and replacing them when necessary.

• Regenerative braking systems can be affected by the temperature and condition of the battery, the speed and weight of the vehicle, and the driving style and terrain. Try avoiding extreme temperature conditions, such as direct sunlight or freezing weather, and park your car in a shaded or covered area. You should also avoid deep discharging or overcharging the battery, and keep it between 20 and 80 percent charged for daily use.

Observing these best practices can help maintain the regenerative braking system and extend its life.

TROUBLESHOOTING COMMON EV PROBLEMS

Troubleshooting common EV problems can be challenging, especially if you are not familiar with the technology and components of electric vehicles. However, there are some common issues that you can identify and fix easily. Here's how you can troubleshoot the most common EV problems:

• Battery issues: The battery is the most important and expensive part of an electric vehicle, and it can also cause some problems if not maintained properly. Some of the battery issues you may encounter are:

o Reduced range or capacity: This means that the battery cannot hold as much charge as it used to, or that it drains faster than normal. This can be caused by various factors, such as age, usage, temperature, charging habits, and calibration. To troubleshoot this issue, you can try to fully charge and balance the battery periodically. You can also check the battery health status on the EV's dashboard or app and see if it needs replacement or repair.

o Charging problems: This means that the battery does not charge properly or at all, or that it takes longer than usual to charge. This can be caused by faulty charging equipment, incompatible charging stations, or damaged battery connectors. To troubleshoot this issue, you can try to use a different charger or cable, check the compatibility of the charging station, and inspect the battery connectors for any signs of corrosion or wear.

o Battery failure: This means that the battery stops working completely, or that it catches fire or explodes. This is a very rare and serious issue that can be caused by manufacturing defects, extreme temperatures, overcharging, physical damage, or water ingress. To troubleshoot this issue, you should stop the vehicle and safely disconnect the battery before looking to service or replace it.

• Coolant issues: The coolant is a liquid that circulates through the battery and the electric motor to keep them from overheating. Some of the coolant issues that you may encounter are:

o Low coolant level: This means that the coolant level is below the recommended range, which can affect the performance and lifespan of the vehicle's battery and motor. This can be caused by leaks, evaporation, or improper filling. To troubleshoot this issue, you can check the coolant level on the EV's dashboard or app and refill it if needed. You should also inspect the coolant system for any signs of leaks or damage and fix them.

o Contaminated coolant: This means that the coolant is dirty, discolored, or mixed with other fluids, which can reduce its effectiveness and cause corrosion or clogging. This can be caused by poor quality coolant, improper mixing, or external contamination. To troubleshoot this issue, you can flush and replace the coolant with the recommended type and amount. You should also clean the coolant system and check for any signs of contamination or damage.

• Brake issues: The brakes are the devices that slow down or stop your EV by applying friction to the wheels. Some of the brake issues that an owner may encounter are:

o Reduced braking performance: This means that the brakes do not respond as quickly or as strongly as they should, or that they make noises or vibrations when applied. This can be caused by worn or damaged brake pads, rotors, calipers, or fluid. To troubleshoot this issue, you can check the brake system for any signs of wear or damage and replace or repair the parts if needed. You should also check the brake fluid level and quality, and refill or change it if needed.

o Regenerative braking failure: This means that the regenerative braking system, which recovers kinetic energy from braking and converts it into electricity, does not work properly or at all. This can reduce your range and efficiency and increase your reliance on conventional brakes. This can be caused by software glitches, sensor failures, or battery issues. To troubleshoot this issue, you can try to reset the EV's computer system, check the sensors for any faults or dirt, and check the battery status and connections.

These are the common EV problems you are most likely to face, and how to troubleshoot and fix them. Note, however, that there may be other issues that are specific to an EV's model or brand, or that require special diagnosis and service.

BATTERY PACK REPLACEMENT

EV batteries are different from conventional car batteries and require some special attention to ensure they perform well and last a long time. However, all batteries will eventually degrade and lose their ability to hold a charge and may need to be replaced after a certain number of years or miles.

The lifespan of an EV battery depends on various factors, such as the type, size, and manufacturer of the battery, the driving and charging habits of the owner, the temperature and climate conditions, and the warranty coverage of the vehicle. According to some sources, the average lifespan of an EV battery ranges from 10 to 20 years, or 100,000 to 200,000 miles. However, this may vary depending on the make and model of the EV, and the situation and care of the battery.

Some signs that indicate that an EV battery may

need to be replaced are:

• The battery capacity drops below 70% of its original level, which means that the battery cannot hold as much charge as it used to, or that it drains faster than normal. This can reduce the range and efficiency of the EV.

• The battery takes unusually long to charge or does not charge at all, which means that the battery has a problem with its charging system, such as faulty connectors, cables, or modules. This can prevent the use of the EV as intended and pose a safety risk.

• The battery overheats to the extent that it becomes a fire hazard, which means that the battery has a problem with its cooling system, such as leaks, clogs, or damage. This can cause the battery to catch fire or explode, which can be very dangerous for the owner and the vehicle.

• The battery gets damaged in an accident, which means that the battery has suffered physical damage from a collision, impact, or puncture. This can compromise the integrity and functionality of the battery, and cause leaks, shorts, or fires.

The average cost of an EV battery pack replacement varies. Some EV owners may not have to pay the full cost of replacing their battery pack, as most EV manufacturers offer a warranty that covers the battery for a certain period of time or mileage. For example, Tesla offers an eight-year warranty with unlimited mileage on the Model S, and Nissan offers an eight-year warranty or 100,000 miles on the Leaf. If the battery fails or degrades below a certain level within the warranty period, the manufacturer will replace it at no extra cost.

Another option that may help EV owners avoid the high cost of replacing their battery pack is to repair it instead. EV battery repair is a growing industry that involves diagnosing and fixing the problems that affect the battery's performance, such as faulty cells, modules, connectors, or wiring. EV battery repair can restore the battery's capacity and extend its lifespan and may cost much less than replacing the entire battery pack.

EV Battery Recycling

The best way to dispose of an EV battery is to recycle it. Recycling EV batteries can help reduce the environmental impact of electric vehicles, conserve valuable materials, and create new economic opportunities. There are different ways to recycle EV batteries, depending on the type, condition, and location of the battery. Here are some options that may be available to you:

- Send to auto recyclers and specialist firms for dismantling and material separation. These companies can take apart the battery packs and separate the different components, such as metals, plastics, wires, and cells. The cells can then be crushed and processed to extract and purify the metals, such as lithium, cobalt, nickel, and manganese. These metals can be reused to make new batteries or other products.

- Use dealership and manufacturer recycling programs, like Toyota's. Some automakers offer recycling programs for their EV batteries, either directly or through partnerships with recyclers. For example, Toyota has a program that collects used hybrid and EV batteries from dealerships and sends them to recyclers. Toyota also works with battery suppliers to design batteries that are easier to recycle and reuse.

- Follow government and industry guidelines for safe disposal. If there are no recycling programs available in your area, you can contact a local hazardous waste disposal facility to see if they accept EV batteries. EV batteries may contain hazardous materials that need to be handled with care and disposed of properly. You should never throw away EV batteries in the trash or recycling bins, as they can cause fires or environmental damage.

Recycling EV batteries is not only good for the environment, but also for the economy. Recycling can create jobs, reduce the dependence on imported materials, and lower the cost of battery production. Recycling can also help meet the growing demand for battery materials, as more electric vehicles are expected to hit the road in the future. Recycling EV batteries is a win-win situation for everyone.

MOTOR AND DRIVE REPAIR

Some common problems you may encounter with EV motors and drives are:

• Abnormal noise or vibration from the motor or the reduction gear. This may indicate a mechanical problem, such as a worn bearing, a loose bolt, or a misaligned shaft. The noise or vibration may also be caused by an electrical problem, such as a faulty sensor, a damaged wire, or a defective inverter.

• Erratic performance or failure of the motor or the drive. This may indicate a problem with the power supply, the motor, the drive, or the communication between them. The problem may be intermittent or permanent, depending on the cause and the severity of the damage. Some examples of motor and drive failures are electrical failure, drive unit replacement, and other faulty components.

• Damage or degradation of the motor or the drive due to external factors, such as heat, moisture, dust, or impact. This may affect the lifespan and the efficiency of the motor and the drive, and may lead to safety hazards, such as fire or electric shock. To prevent or minimize the damage, the motor and drive need to be properly installed, ventilated, protected, and insulated.

These problems can affect the reliability, performance, and safety of EVs, and may require specialized tools and methods to diagnose and fix. Signs of a failing EV motor or drive are:

• Overheating: If the motor is consistently overheating or hot to the touch, it may indicate a problem with the fan, the ventilation, the insulation, or the power supply. Overheating can damage the motor winding insulation and reduce its lifespan.

• Vibration and unusual noises: If the motor is vibrating more than usual or making abnormal noises, such as whining, grinding, or squealing, it may indicate a problem with the bearings, the shaft, the rotor, the stator, or the wiring. Vibration and noise can affect the motor performance and efficiency.

• Frequent tripping of circuit breakers: If the electric motor frequently causes circuit breakers to trip or fuses to blow, it may indicate a problem with the power supply, the motor, the drive, or the communication between them. Tripping of circuit breakers can interrupt the motor operation and cause safety hazards.

• Decreased performance and efficiency: If the motor is not delivering the expected torque, speed, or power, or if it is consuming more energy than usual, it may indicate a problem with the motor parameters, the drive settings, the fault codes, or the external factors. Decreased performance and efficiency can affect the reliability and cost of the motor operation.

• Excessive energy consumption: If the motor is using more energy than it should, it may indicate a problem with the motor efficiency, the power factor, the load, or the voltage. Excessive energy consumption can increase the operating cost and the environmental impact of the motor operation.

• Irregular motor operation: If the motor is not starting, stopping, or running smoothly, it may indicate a problem with the motor control, the drive control, the sensors, or the feedback. Irregular motor operation can affect the motor functionality and safety.

Servicing motors and drives is an important aspect of electric car maintenance and helps optimize the performance and safety of the vehicle. Here are some of the things technicians need to know about servicing EV motors and drives:

• EV motors and drives consist of the electric motor that propels the vehicle, the power electronics that control the motor, and the reduction gear that transfers the torque to the wheels. These components are usually integrated into a single unit, called the EV motor drive unit.

• EV motors and drives require less maintenance than internal combustion engines, as they have fewer moving parts and no oil or spark plugs to change. However, they still need to be checked for abnormal noise, vibration, performance, or failure, which may indicate a mechanical or electrical problem.

• EV motors and drives may also be affected by external factors, such as heat, moisture, dust, or impact, which can damage or degrade the components and reduce their lifespan and efficiency. To prevent or minimize the damage, the EV motor drive unit and reduction gear need to be properly installed, ventilated, protected, and insulated.

EV motors and drives may need to be serviced by a qualified technician, who can use specialized tools and methods to diagnose and fix the problems. Some of the tools and methods include a multimeter, an oscilloscope, a thermal imager, or a motor-drive analyzer, as well as checking the motor parameters, the drive settings, and the fault codes.

EV motors and drives may have different service intervals and procedures, depending on the make and model of the vehicle. You should consult the vehicle's owner's manual or the manufacturer's website to find out the recommended maintenance schedule and guidelines for your EV. Some examples of service intervals and procedures are:

• Tesla: Tesla recommends servicing the EV motor drive unit and reduction gear every two years or 25,000 miles, whichever comes first. The service includes a cabin air filter change, a brake fluid test, and an inspection of the motor and drive components.

• Nissan: Nissan recommends servicing the EV motor drive unit and reduction gear every 12 months or 18,000 miles, whichever comes first. The service includes a brake fluid change, a cabin air filter change, and an inspection of the motor and drive components.

• Chevrolet: Chevrolet recommends servicing the EV motor drive unit and reduction gear every 7,500 miles. The service includes a tire rotation, a cabin air filter change, and an inspection of the motor and drive components.

Servicing EV motors and drives is a vital skill for technicians as it can extend the life of these components and avoid unnecessary replacements.

Moving On...

It this chapter, we have learned about the routine maintenance tasks for EVs, troubleshooting common EV problems, battery pack replacement, and repairing EV motors and drives. In the next chapter we will dive into some advanced EV topics that technicians need to know about.

6 ADVANCED EV TOPICS

Learning about advanced EV technologies will help EV technicians better understand how these technologies work and how to troubleshoot potential problems resulting from their use. EV technicians who have knowledge of advanced EV technologies and topics will be in high demand, command higher wages, and are more likely to advance in their careers.

In this chapter, we will discuss some advanced EV topics like:

- Vehicle-to-grid (V2G) technology
- Solar-powered EVs
- Autonomous EVs
- Other emerging technologies

Let's begin by examining vehicle-to-grid (V2G)

technology.

VEHICLE-TO-GRID (V2G) TECHNOLOGY

What is vehicle-to-grid technology? Vehicle-to-grid (V2G) technology is a system that allows electric vehicles to communicate and interact with the electrical grid. This means that EVs can not only receive electricity from the grid but can also send electricity back to the grid.

How Does It Work?

V2G technology enables electric vehicles to either charge their batteries from the grid or discharge their stored energy back to the grid when needed. V2G technology works as follows:

• The electric vehicle is connected to a bidirectional charger, which can either supply electricity to the vehicle or draw electricity from the vehicle. The bidirectional charger is also connected to the power grid and a smart meter, which measures the electricity flow and usage.

• The power grid sends signals to the bidirectional charger, indicating the current and projected demand and supply of electricity. The signals can be based on various factors, such as the time of day, the weather, the price of electricity, and the availability of renewable energy sources.

• The bidirectional charger responds to the signals by either charging or discharging the electric vehicle's battery, depending on the optimal scenario for both the grid and the vehicle owner. For example, the charger may charge the vehicle when the electricity demand is low and the price is cheap, or discharge the vehicle when the electricity demand is high and the price is expensive.

• The smart meter records the amount of electricity that is exchanged between the vehicle and the grid, and calculates the net cost or benefit for the vehicle owner. The vehicle owner may receive payments or incentives from the grid operator or the utility company for providing electricity or ancillary services to the grid.

Benefits

V2G technology has many benefits, such as:

• It can help balance the power grid and integrate more renewable energy sources, by providing flexible and distributed energy storage and generation.

• It can reduce the greenhouse gas emissions and air pollution from the transportation and the electricity sectors, by using clean and renewable energy sources instead of fossil fuels.

• It can save money and generate income for the electric vehicle owners, by optimizing the charging and discharging patterns and participating in the electricity markets or grid services.

• It can increase the reliability and resilience of the power grid and the electric vehicle, by providing backup power and emergency services in case of blackouts or disasters.

Limitations

There are some drawbacks to V2G technology, which include:

• Battery degradation. V2G technology requires frequent charging and discharging of the electric vehicle's battery, which may reduce its capacity and lifespan over time. This may increase the maintenance and replacement costs of the battery, and affect the performance and reliability of the vehicle.

• Charger and communication efficiency. V2G technology requires bidirectional chargers and smart meters that can supply or draw electricity from the vehicle and communicate with the grid. However, these devices may have high costs, losses, and limited efficiency, which may reduce the net benefits of V2G technology. Moreover, these devices may not be compatible or interoperable with different vehicles, chargers, and grids, which may create confusion and inconsistency among the users and the authorities.

• Aggregation. V2G technology requires a large number of electric vehicles to participate and coordinate with the grid, which may be difficult to achieve and manage. Electric vehicle owners may have different preferences, behaviors, and incentives for using V2G technology, which may affect their availability and willingness to provide electricity or ancillary services to the grid. Furthermore, there may be ethical and social issues that need to be addressed, such as the impact of V2G technology on the economy, the infrastructure, and the society.

Overall, V2G technology has the potential to play a significant role in the transition to a clean and sustainable energy future. Here are some examples of how V2G technology could be used:

• A homeowner with an EV could use V2G technology to power their home during a power outage.

• A business with a fleet of EVs could use V2G technology to sell electricity back to the grid during peak hours.

• A utility company could use V2G technology to store excess renewable energy and then discharge that electricity back to the grid when it is needed.

V2G technology is still in its early stages of development, but there are a number of pilot projects underway around the world. As the technology matures and becomes more cost-effective, we can expect to see V2G technology become more widely adopted.

SOLAR-POWERED EVs

Solar-powered EVs, also known as solar electric vehicles (SEVs), are vehicles that use solar power to generate electricity to power their electric motors. SEVs typically have solar panels mounted on their roofs or bodies, which convert sunlight into electricity. This electricity is then stored in a battery, which powers the vehicle's motor.

How They Work

SEVs are vehicles that use solar energy to power their electric motors. They have solar panels on the car roof or other surfaces that collect energy from the sun. This energy is then converted into electricity and stored in the car's battery. The electric motor uses this electricity to power the car.

There are different types of solar powered electric

vehicles, depending on the design and efficiency of the solar panels and the battery. Some solar powered electric vehicles can run entirely on solar energy, while others use solar energy as a supplementary source of power. Some solar powered electric vehicles are also hybrid vehicles, which can switch between solar power and another fuel source, such as gasoline or hydrogen.

Benefits

SEVs have many benefits, such as:

• They can save money on fuel, as they do not need to rely on gasoline or diesel. They can also use the electricity from their own solar panels or from public charging stations that have installed onsite solar panels.

• They are sustainable and eco-friendly, as they use clean and renewable energy sources instead of fossil fuels. They can reduce greenhouse gas emissions and air pollution, and improve environmental health.

• They have low maintenance costs, as they have fewer moving parts and less wear and tear than internal combustion engines. They only need to replace their batteries periodically.

• They do not cause noise pollution or air pollution, as they operate quietly and smoothly. They also improve the comfort and safety of the passengers and the drivers.

Limitations

SEVs are not very common yet, as they face some challenges and limitations, such as:

• The availability and efficiency of solar panels, which depend on the weather, the location, and the design of the vehicle. Solar panels may not be able to provide enough power for long-distance travel or high-speed driving.

• The cost and performance of batteries, which affect the range, speed, and durability of the vehicle. Batteries may also pose a risk of fire or explosion if they overheat or malfunction.

• The lack of standardization and regulation, which create confusion and inconsistency among the users and the authorities. There are also ethical and social issues that need to be addressed, such as the impact of solar powered vehicles on the economy, the infrastructure, and the society.

New research and innovation in solar technology and battery technology may help solve these problems and improve the feasibility and popularity of solar powered electric vehicles in the future.

SEVs are still in their early stages of development, but a number of companies are developing and producing SEVs for commercial sale. Some of the most well-known examples of SEVs include the following:

• Sono Sion: The Sono Sion is a five-seater hatchback that is expected to enter production in 2023. The Sion has 465 integrated solar half-cells on its exterior, which can provide an additional 15-45 miles of range per day.

• Lightyear 0: The Lightyear 0 is a luxury sedan that is expected to enter production in 2023. The Lightyear 0 has solar panels on its roof and hood, which can provide up to 43 miles of range per day.

• Aptera: The Aptera is a two-seater vehicle that is expected to enter production in 2023. The Aptera has solar panels on its entire body, which can provide up to 40 miles of range per day.

While SEVs are still more expensive than traditional vehicles, the cost of SEVs is expected to come down in the coming years. As SEVs become more affordable and widely available, they are likely to play a significant role in the transition to a clean and sustainable transportation system.

AUTONOMOUS EVs

Autonomous EVs are electric vehicles that can drive themselves without human intervention. They use various sensors, cameras, and artificial intelligence to perceive the environment, plan the route, and control the vehicle. Autonomous EVs have the potential to reduce greenhouse gas emissions, improve road safety, and provide mobility and convenience to passengers.

Some examples of autonomous EVs are:

• The Turing EV, a fully autonomous electric car that uses artificial intelligence imaging and scanning to drive around highways and cities.

• The Chevrolet Bolt, an all-electric vehicle that GM's Cruise has been testing for self-driving in San Francisco.

• The Ford Fusion Hybrid, a gas-electric hybrid vehicle that Ford plans to use for its autonomous vehicle service in 2022.

How Do They Work?

The basic working principle of autonomous EVs is as follows:

• The battery provides the power for the electric motor, which drives the wheels. The battery can be recharged by plugging into a charging station or by regenerative braking, which captures kinetic energy when the vehicle decelerates.

•   The sensors collect data about the surrounding environment, such as the distance and speed of other vehicles, pedestrians, traffic signs, road markings, and obstacles. The sensors include cameras, radars, lidars, ultrasonic sensors, and GPS.

•   The computer processes the sensor data and uses artificial intelligence algorithms to make decisions about how to control the vehicle. The computer also communicates with other vehicles and infrastructure through wireless networks, such as 5G or V2X (vehicle-to-everything).

•   The actuators execute the commands from the computer, such as steering, accelerating, braking, and signaling. The actuators are connected to the electric motor, the brakes, the steering wheel, and the lights.

Benefits

Some benefits of autonomous EVs are:

•   They can reduce greenhouse gas emissions and air pollution by using clean and renewable energy sources instead of fossil fuels.

•   They can improve road safety and reduce traffic accidents by using advanced sensors, cameras, and artificial intelligence to avoid collisions, obey traffic rules, and adapt to changing road conditions.

• They can provide mobility and convenience to passengers by allowing them to relax, work, or entertain themselves while traveling, and by offering personalized and on-demand transportation services.

Limitations

Autonomous EVs face some challenges, such as the limited range of electric batteries, the high energy consumption of self-driving software and sensors, and the regulatory and ethical issues of autonomous driving. However, new research and innovation in computing and battery technology may help overcome these obstacles and make autonomous EVs more feasible and widespread in the future.

Risks

There are certain risks associated with self-driving vehicles. Some of them can be described as follows:

• False sense of security. Some self-driving cars are marketed as "driverless", which may lead human drivers to act more like passive passengers and become distracted or disengaged from the driving task. However, none of the current self-driving cars are fully autonomous, and they still require human supervision and intervention in some situations. This may create a gap between the expectations and the reality of self-driving cars, and increase the risk of accidents.

• Danger of fire. Self-driving cars use lithium-ion batteries, which are highly combustible and can cause intense and prolonged fires. This may pose a threat to the occupants and the emergency responders, especially if the self-driving car is involved in a crash or a malfunction.

• Lack of standardization and regulation. Self-driving cars are a new and rapidly evolving technology, and there is no clear and consistent framework for testing, certifying, and regulating them. Different automakers and tech companies may have different approaches and levels of autonomy for their self-driving cars, which may create confusion and inconsistency among the users and the authorities. Moreover, there are ethical and legal issues that need to be addressed, such as the liability and accountability of self-driving cars in case of accidents, the privacy and security of the data collected by self-driving cars, and the social and economic impacts of self-driving cars on the society.

OTHER EMERGING EV TECHNOLOGIES

In addition to V2G technology, solar powered and autonomous driving EVs, there are some other exciting areas of advanced EV technologies on the horizon, such as solid-state batteries, graphene supercapacitors, silicon carbide and wireless charging. A brief description of each of these exciting new technologies follows.

Solid-State Batteries

Solid state batteries are a type of advanced battery technology that uses solid materials instead of liquid electrolytes to store and transfer electric charge. Solid state batteries have several advantages over conventional lithium-ion batteries, such as higher energy density, faster charging, longer lifespan, and lower fire risk. Solid state batteries could revolutionize the performance and safety of electric vehicles, as well as enable new applications such as wireless charging and dynamic charging.

However, solid state batteries are still in the early stages of development and face some challenges, such as high cost, complex manufacturing, limited availability, and durability issues. Many automakers and startups are working on developing and commercializing solid state batteries for EVs, such as Toyota, Honda, Hyundai, BMW, Ford, GM, Volkswagen, WiTricity, and Char.gy. Some of them have announced plans to launch EVs with solid state batteries by 2025 or later.

Graphene Supercapacitors

Graphene supercapacitors are a type of energy storage device that can charge and discharge faster, last longer, and perform better than conventional batteries. Graphene is a thin layer of carbon atoms arranged in a hexagonal lattice, which has remarkable electrical, thermal, and mechanical properties. Graphene supercapacitors use graphene as the electrode material, which can increase the surface area, conductivity, and capacitance of the device. Graphene supercapacitors can store more energy, deliver more power, and withstand more cycles than batteries, making them ideal for applications that require high performance and reliability, such as electric vehicles.

Graphene supercapacitors can offer several benefits for electric vehicles, such as:

• Extending the driving range and battery life of EVs by providing additional energy and reducing the stress on the battery.

• Reducing the charging time and improving the efficiency of EVs by enabling fast and wireless charging.

• Enhancing the safety and sustainability of

EVs by eliminating the risk of fire, explosion, or leakage of toxic materials that may occur with batteries.

• Lowering the cost and environmental impact of EVs by using less materials, resources, and energy to produce and operate graphene supercapacitors.

Graphene supercapacitors are still a developing technology, with some challenges and opportunities for innovation and commercialization. Some of the challenges include the high cost and complexity of graphene production, the limited availability and quality of graphene materials, and the need for standardization and regulation of graphene devices. Some of the opportunities include the increasing demand and investment for graphene technology, the potential for collaboration and partnership among different stakeholders, and the possibility of creating new value propositions and business models for EVs.

Silicon Carbide (SiC) Semiconductors

Silicon carbide (SiC) semiconductors are a type of advanced materials that can improve the performance, efficiency, and reliability of electric vehicles (EVs). SiC semiconductors have several advantages over traditional silicon (Si) semiconductors, such as higher switching frequency, thermal resistance, and breakdown voltage. These characteristics enable SiC semiconductors to reduce the size, weight, and cost of the power electronics in EVs, such as inverters, converters, and chargers. SiC semiconductors can also extend the range and battery life of EVs, as well as reduce the charging time and the cooling requirements.

SiC semiconductors are expected to play a key role in the growth of the EV market, which is projected to reach 64 million units by 2030, with 75% of them being battery electric vehicles (BEVs). SiC semiconductors are especially suitable for high-voltage BEVs, which can offer faster charging and longer driving distances than low-voltage BEVs. SiC semiconductors are also compatible with wireless charging technology, which can provide convenience and safety for EV drivers.

SiC semiconductors are still an emerging technology, with some challenges and opportunities for manufacturers, suppliers, and automakers. Some of the challenges include the high cost and complexity of SiC production, the limited availability and quality of SiC wafers, and the need for standardization and regulation of SiC devices. Some of the opportunities include the increasing demand

and innovation for SiC devices, the potential for collaboration and partnership among different stakeholders, and the possibility of creating new value propositions and business models for EVs.

Wireless Charging

Wireless charging is another exciting and innovative technology that could change the way we power our vehicles. Wireless charging technology is a type of wireless power transfer that uses electromagnetic induction to provide electricity to portable devices without plugging in a cable. Wireless charging for EVs works by transferring energy between two magnetic coils: one on the charging pad, which is connected to the power supply and is located on the ground, and the other on the charging receiver inside the vehicle. The EV is charged wirelessly, transmitting energy from the charger to the vehicle battery.

Wireless charging for EVs has several benefits, such as convenience, safety, and efficiency. Wireless charging eliminates the need for drivers to plug in their vehicles, which can be especially handy in bad weather or for on-street parking. Wireless charging also reduces the risk of electric shock, fire, or vandalism that may occur with wired charging.

Wireless charging can also improve the efficiency of EVs by reducing battery degradation and enabling dynamic charging while driving.

Wireless charging for EVs is still a nascent market with a lot of potential to grow. Some startups are developing wireless charging technology for EVs, such as WiTricity, which licenses its magnetic resonance wireless charging tech to suppliers and automakers. WiTricity's technology debuted on the Hyundai Genesis GV60 in South Korea in October 2023. Another startup is Char.gy, which is running a 12-month trial in the UK with 10 wireless charging pads installed in public parking spaces for a fleet of 10 Renault Zoe cars modified to work with the wireless chargers.

EV technologies are constantly evolving, and EV technicians need to be able to keep up with the latest trends and developments in order to properly service and repair EVs. Some companies offer training programs on advanced EV technologies, and there are a number of online and in-person courses available to help EV technicians stay abreast with advanced EV topics. There are many industry publications and websites that cover EV technologies, and there are conferences and events that focus on advanced EV topics.

Moving On...

It this chapter, our focus has been on some of the hottest EV technologies on the horizon. In the next chapter, we will examine opportunities for career advancement for EV technicians.

7 CAREER ADVANCEMENT

The future prospect for an EV technician career is promising, with a projected growth rate of 6%, much faster than the average for all occupations. This growth is driven by the increasing popularity of electric vehicles and the need for qualified technicians to service and repair them.

IN this chapter, we will look at the prospect for career advancement for EV technicians. We will discuss:
- Opportunities for advancement, and
- Continuing education and professional development

Let's begin by looking at some ways to advance your career as an EV technician.

OPPORTUNITIES FOR ADVANCEMENT

There are many opportunities for career advancement for EV technicians, depending on your skills, interests, and goals. Here are some possible paths you can take to advance your career in the electric vehicle industry:

- Pursue further education or certification. You can enhance your knowledge and skills by taking courses, workshops, or online programs related to electric vehicle technology, such as battery systems, electric motors, charging infrastructure, or software development. You can also obtain certifications from industry associations or manufacturers that demonstrate your proficiency and expertise in specific areas of electric vehicle service or repair.

- Seek promotion or leadership roles within your organization. You can apply for higher-level positions that involve more responsibility, authority, or supervision of other technicians or staff. You can also take on additional tasks or projects that showcase your initiative, creativity, or problem-solving skills.

- Explore opportunities in other sectors or industries related to electric vehicles. You can use your skills and experience to work in different settings or fields that involve electric vehicle technology, such as research and development, manufacturing, infrastructure development, or sales and support. You can also work for organizations that provide services or products for electric vehicles, such as battery suppliers, charging station operators, or software developers.

• Start your own business or venture. You can leverage your entrepreneurial spirit and passion for electric vehicles to create your own opportunities or solutions for the electric vehicle market. You can start your own service or repair shop, develop your own electric vehicle products or applications, or offer your own consulting or training services for electric vehicle owners or enthusiasts.

These are just some of the possible ways you can advance your career as an EV technician. You can also network with other professionals, join industry associations, or attend events or conferences to learn more about the latest trends, innovations, or opportunities in the electric vehicle industry. Whatever path you choose, you can enjoy a rewarding and exciting career in this fast-growing and dynamic field.

Become A Specialist

EV technicians with specialized skills are in high demand. If you are interested in advancing your career as an EV technician, consider specializing in a particular area to increase your job opportunities and earning potential. Here are some areas of specialization for EV technicians:

• Battery systems: EV technicians who specialize in battery systems are responsible for diagnosing and repairing battery problems. They may also work on developing new battery technologies.

• Charging systems: EV technicians who specialize in charging systems are responsible for diagnosing and repairing problems with EV charging stations and charging equipment. They may also work on developing new charging technologies.

• Electric motors and powertrains: EV technicians who specialize in electric motors and powertrains are responsible for diagnosing and repairing problems with EV motors and drivetrains. They may also work on developing new electric motor and powertrain technologies.

• Diagnostics and repair: EV technicians who specialize in diagnostics and repair are responsible for diagnosing and repairing all aspects of EVs, including battery systems, charging systems, electric motors, powertrains, and other electrical components.

• Software and firmware: EV technicians who

specialize in software and firmware are responsible for diagnosing and repairing problems with EV software and firmware. They may also work on developing new EV software and firmware technologies.

EV technicians may also specialize in a particular type of EV, such as passenger cars, commercial vehicles, or heavy-duty vehicles. In addition, EV technicians may consider becoming a specialist in:

• EV fleet maintenance: EV technicians who specialize in EV fleet maintenance are responsible for maintaining and repairing fleets of electric vehicles. This may involve working on a variety of EV models and makes.

• EV charging infrastructure: EV technicians who specialize in EV charging infrastructure are responsible for installing, maintaining, and repairing EV charging stations.

• EV research and development: EV technicians who specialize in EV research and development work on developing new EV technologies, such as battery systems, charging systems, electric motors, and powertrains.

Become A Lead Technician

Becoming a lead EV technician is a great way to

demonstrate your status as a competent and experienced service technician. To become a lead tech, you will need to acquire several skills and qualifications, for example:

• A certificate or degree in electric vehicle technology, automotive technology, or a related field. You can find some online programs that offer electric vehicle technician training, such as the Electric Vehicle (EV) Technician Certificate Program or the Electric Vehicle Technology Certificate program from Sills Commons.

• Experience in repairing and servicing electric vehicles, including hybrid, plug-in hybrid, and all-electric vehicles. You can gain experience by completing an internship or working as an entry-level technician at an auto manufacturer, dealer, or repair shop that specializes in electric vehicles.

• Certification from the National Institute for Automotive Service Excellence (ASE) in relevant areas, such as electrical/electronic systems, engine performance, and hybrid/electric vehicle systems. You can also pursue the ASE master status by passing all eight tests in the automobile series. ASE certification demonstrates your competence and professionalism as an electric vehicle technician.

• Knowledge of the components and types of electric vehicles, such as batteries, electric motors, internal combustion engines, and charging systems.

• Skills in diagnosing, troubleshooting, and repairing electric vehicle problems, using specialized tools and equipment, such as multimeters, oscilloscopes, and battery testers. You should also be familiar with the safety procedures and regulations for working with high-voltage systems.

• Leadership and communication skills to supervise and train other technicians, coordinate with customers and suppliers, and ensure quality and efficiency of the work. You should also be able to work independently and as part of a team.

Become A Charging Station Installer

As a career advancement option, you may consider becoming a charging station installer. To become one, you need to:

• Get licensed as an electrician. In most states, you will need to be a licensed electrician to install EV charging stations. The licensing requirements vary by state, so be sure to check the requirements in your state.

• Complete EV charging station installer training. There are a number of organizations that offer EV charging station installer training programs. These programs typically cover topics such as EV charging station theory, installation procedures, safety, and troubleshooting.

• Get certified as an EV charging station installer. There are a number of organizations that offer EV charging station installer certifications. One popular certification is the Electric Vehicle Charging Station Certified Installer (EVCS-CI) certification from the National Electrical Contractors Association (NECA). To get certified as an EVCS-CI, you must pass a written exam and have at least two years of experience working as an electrician.

Once you have completed the necessary training and certification, you will be qualified to install and maintain EV charging stations. You can work for an electrical contracting company, an EV charging station installation company, or start your own business.

Open Your Own Repair Shop

If you are interested in opening your own repair shop as an EV technician, you will need to follow some steps to plan, launch, and grow your venture. Here are some of the main steps you should follow:

• Plan your business: You should have a clear idea of what services you will offer, who your target market is, how you will differentiate yourself from competitors, and how you will finance your business.

You should also conduct market research and analysis to validate your business idea and identify your opportunities and challenges.

• Form a legal entity: You should choose a business structure that suits your needs and protects you from personal liability. Some of the common options are sole proprietorship, partnership, limited liability company (LLC), and corporation. You should also register your business name and obtain any necessary licenses and permits for your state and local area.

• Register for taxes: You will need to register for various state and federal taxes before you can open your business. Depending on your business structure, you may need to apply for an Employer Identification Number (EIN), which is also known as a Federal Tax Identification Number. You should also be aware of the sales tax, income tax, and payroll tax requirements for your business.

• Open a business bank account and credit card: You should separate your personal and business finances by opening a dedicated bank account and credit card for your business. This will help you keep track of your income and expenses, as well as make it easier to file your taxes and report your financial performance.

• Set up business accounting: You should

record your various sources of income and expenses on a regular basis, using a reliable accounting software or system. This will help you monitor the financial health of your business, as well as prepare your financial statements and tax returns.

• Obtain necessary permits and licenses: You should comply with the federal, state, and local regulations that apply to your business, such as zoning, safety, environmental, and vehicle standards. You should also obtain any specific permits and licenses that are required for electric vehicle conversion, such as the Electric Vehicle Technician (EVT) certification from the Electronics Technicians Association (ETA).

• Get business insurance: You should protect your business from potential risks and liabilities by obtaining the appropriate insurance policies, such as general liability insurance, workers' compensation insurance, and commercial auto insurance. You should also consider getting professional liability insurance, which covers you in case of errors or negligence in your services.

• Define your brand: You should create a unique and memorable identity for your business, which reflects your mission, vision, values, and personality. You should also design a logo, slogan, and color scheme that represent your brand and appeal to your target audience.

• Create your business website: You should have a professional and user-friendly website that showcases your services, portfolio, testimonials, and contact information. You should also optimize your website for search engines, mobile devices, and social media platforms, to increase your online visibility and reach.

• Set up your business phone system: You should have a reliable and secure phone system that allows you to communicate with your customers, suppliers, and partners. You should also choose a phone number that is easy to remember and reflects your brand and location.

Consider A Franchise

A franchise electric vehicle repair shop is a business that operates under a license from an established brand, such as Tesla, Ford, or Toyota. A franchisee pays a fee and agrees to follow certain standards and guidelines set by the franchisor, such as using their name, logo, equipment, and parts. A franchise electric vehicle repair shop benefits from the brand recognition, marketing, training, and support of the franchisor, but also has to share a percentage of its revenue and adhere to their rules and regulations.

In contrast, an independent electric vehicle repair shop is a business that operates on its own, without any affiliation to a specific brand or manufacturer. An independent repair shop has more freedom and flexibility in choosing its name, location, equipment, and parts, but also has to compete with other shops and dealerships for customers and reputation. An independent repair shop can offer lower prices, faster service, and more personalized attention, but also has to invest more in advertising, training, and certification.

Some of the main differences between a franchise and an independent electric vehicle repair shop are:

• Cost: A franchise electric vehicle repair shop typically has higher costs than an independent one, due to the fees, royalties, and expenses associated with the franchise agreement. A franchise electric vehicle repair shop also has to use only original equipment manufacturer (OEM) parts, which are usually more expensive than aftermarket or refurbished parts. An independent electric vehicle repair shop can save money by using cheaper or alternative parts, as long as they meet the quality and safety standards.

• Quality: A franchise electric vehicle repair

shop typically has higher quality than an independent one, due to the training, certification, and warranty provided by the franchisor. A franchise electric vehicle repair shop also has access to the latest tools, technology, and data from the manufacturer, which can help diagnose and fix problems more accurately and efficiently. An independent electric vehicle repair shop may have less expertise and experience in working with electric vehicles, especially newer or more complex models, and may not have the same level of warranty or customer service.

• Availability: A franchise electric vehicle repair shop typically has lower availability than an independent one, due to the limited number and location of the franchised outlets. A franchise electric vehicle repair shop may also have longer waiting times and appointments, due to the high demand and volume of customers. An independent electric vehicle repair shop can offer more convenience and accessibility, as they can operate in any area and cater to any customer. An independent electric vehicle repair shop may also have shorter turnaround times and more flexible schedules.

Working For an Auto Manufacturer

There are many benefits for an EV technician to consider working for an EV manufacturer. Here are some to think about:

• Job security: EV manufacturers are growing rapidly, so there is a high demand for skilled EV technicians. This means that EV technicians typically have good job security and plenty of opportunities for advancement.

• Competitive salaries: EV manufacturers typically offer competitive salaries and benefits packages to their employees. This includes things like health insurance, retirement plans, and paid time off.

• Opportunities for training and development: EV manufacturers are often at the forefront of EV technology, so their technicians have access to the latest training and development opportunities. This helps technicians stay up-to-date on the latest EV technologies and skills.

• Opportunities to work on cutting-edge EV technologies: EV manufacturers are constantly developing new EV technologies, so their technicians have the opportunity to work on some of the most innovative EV technologies in the world.

Some additional benefits of working for an EV manufacturer include:

• Opportunity to make a real difference: Working for an EV manufacturer gives technicians the opportunity to make a real difference in the fight against climate change. EVs are a key part of the transition to a clean energy future, so technicians who work on EVs are helping to make the world a better place.

• Supportive work environment: EV manufacturers are often known for having supportive and collaborative work environments. This can be a great benefit for technicians who are looking to learn and grow.

• Opportunities to travel: EV manufacturers may have offices and factories all over the world, so technicians may have the opportunity to travel for work. This can be a great way to experience different cultures and learn about different EV markets.

Working for an EV manufacturer is a great way to achieve your career objectives while experiencing a supportive and collaborative work environment. EV manufacturers typically have high standards for their employees, so technicians may need to be prepared for a challenging work environment. Additionally, EV manufacturers may be located in remote areas, so technicians may need to be willing to relocate.

CONTINUING EDUCATION AND PROFESSIONAL DEVELOPMENT

Continuing education is essential for EV technicians to stay up-to-date on the latest technologies and repair procedures. There are a number of specific organizations that offer continuing education for EV technicians. These include:

• National Alternative Fuels Training Consortium (NAFTC): The NAFTC offers a variety of EV training programs for technicians and students, including online courses, in-person training, and certifications.

• FutureTech EVPro+ training program: This program provides comprehensive training on electric, hybrid, and plug-in vehicle systems and technologies.

• National Institute for Automotive Service Excellence (ASE): ASE offers a number of EV technician certifications, including the ASE Hybrid/Electric Vehicle Specialist certification.

• National Automotive Technicians Education Foundation (NATEF): NATEF offers a number of EV technician certifications, including the NATEF EV/HEV Specialist certification.

• Society of Automotive Engineers (SAE): SAE offers a number of EV training courses and certifications.

In addition to these organizations, many EV

manufacturers and aftermarket companies also offer continuing education programs for EV technicians. When choosing a continuing education program, it is important to consider:

• Topics covered: Make sure the program covers the topics that are most relevant to your work.

• Instructor qualifications: Choose a program taught by experienced and qualified instructors.

• Cost: Compare the cost of different programs to find one that fits your budget.

• Flexibility: Choose a program that offers flexible scheduling options, so you can fit it into your work schedule.

By taking advantage of continuing education opportunities, EV technicians can stay up-to-date on the latest developments in the EV service industry and provide their customers with the best possible service.

Professional Development Opportunities

EV technicians should take advantage of professional development opportunities to stay ahead of the curve. Here are some specific opportunities for you to consider:

• SAE International Electric Vehicle Technician Certification: This certification program is designed to validate the skills and knowledge of EV technicians. Upon successful completion of the certification exam, technicians will earn the title of SAE Certified Electric Vehicle Technician.

• ASE Hybrid/Electric Vehicle Specialist Certification: This certification program is designed to assess the skills and knowledge of technicians who diagnose, service, and repair hybrid and electric vehicles. Upon successful completion of the certification exam, technicians will earn the title of ASE Certified Hybrid/Electric Vehicle Specialist.

• National Alternative Fuels Training Consortium (NAFTC) EV Technician Training Program: This program provides technicians with the skills and knowledge they need to diagnose, service, and repair electric vehicles. The program covers a variety of topics, including EV basics, high-voltage safety, and specific EV systems and components.

• FutureTech EVPro+ training program: This program provides comprehensive training on electric, hybrid, and plug-in vehicle systems and technologies. The program is designed for technicians who want to specialize in EV repair and maintenance.

There are other ways for EV technicians to pursue professional development. For example, technicians can read industry publications, attend webinars, and network with other EV professionals online and in person.

Professional Associations

There are many professional associations that EV technicians can join and learn from. Here are some organizations that you should look up:

• The Electric Auto Association (EAA) is a nonprofit organization that promotes and supports the adoption of electric vehicles in North America. It has over 80 chapters and thousands of members who share their experiences and knowledge about driving electric. Members of the EAA receive the monthly "Current EVents" magazine and have access to various resources and events. You can find more information about the EAA on their website.

• The World Electric Vehicle Association (WEVA) is a global organization that aims to advance the research, development, and deployment of electric drive vehicles. WEVA organizes the International Electric Vehicle Symposium (EVS) series, the World Electric Vehicle Journal, and the E-Visionary Award. WEVA consists of three regional associations: the Electric Drive Transportation Association (EDTA), the European Association for Battery, Hybrid and Fuel Cell Electric Vehicles (AVERE), and the Electric Vehicle Association of

Asia Pacific (EVAAP). You can learn more about WEVA and its activities on their website.

• The EVPRO+ is a training program for automotive and transportation service professionals who want to upgrade their skills and knowledge on electric vehicles. EVPRO+ offers a blended learning approach that combines online courses, hands-on workshops, and certification exams. EVPRO+ covers topics such as EV fundamentals, diagnostics, maintenance, repair, and safety. You can read more about EVPRO+ and how to enroll by going to their website.

Resources

Many resources are available to help EV technicians stay current. Examples include:

• National Alternative Fuels Training Consortium (NAFTC): The NAFTC offers a variety of EV training programs for technicians and students.

• FutureTech EVPro+ training program: This program provides comprehensive training on electric, hybrid, and plug-in vehicle systems and technologies.

• EVSE.com: This website is a valuable resource for EV charging station technicians. It includes news, articles, and training resources.

• Electric Vehicle Charging Association

(EVCA): The EVCA is a trade association that represents the EV charging industry. It offers a variety of resources for EV charging station technicians, including training programs and webinars.

To summarize, the demand for skilled EV technicians is expected to increase in the coming years. Upskilling in EV technology can help EV technicians advance their careers, as they can move into more senior positions or start their own businesses. Skilled EV technicians earn higher salaries than traditional auto technicians, as they have more specialized knowledge and experience in working with electric vehicles. EV technicians can pursue training, specialization, and certification in relevant areas, such as the Electric Vehicle Technician (EVT) certification from the Electronics Technicians Association (ETA) or the ASE master status from the National Institute for Automotive Service Excellence (ASE). These steps will help technicians remain sharp and become more marketable in the ever-expanding EV industry.

8 CONCLUSION

Congratulations on completing this book on how to become an EV service technician! You have now taken the first step towards a rewarding and exciting career in the rapidly growing EV industry.

In this book, you have learned about the skills and knowledge required for the job, and the steps you can take to become an EV technician. You have also learned about the different types of EV vehicles and the different components that make them up.

Now that you have a good understanding of the basics, it is time to start putting your knowledge into practice. The best way to learn how to become an EV technician is to get hands-on experience. You can do this by getting a job at an EV dealership or repair shop, or by volunteering to work on EVs with a local EV club or organization.

As you gain experience, you will also want to continue your education by taking training courses and workshops on EV technology. There are many different training providers that offer courses on EV repair and maintenance. You can also find online courses and tutorials that can help you learn more about EV technology.

Here are some recommendations for success as an EV service technician:

• Get certified. There are a number of different EV technician certifications available. Getting certified can help you demonstrate your skills and knowledge to potential employers.

• Be customer-oriented. EV owners are investing in the future of transportation, and they expect to receive high-quality service from their EV technicians. Be professional and courteous in your interactions with customers, and always go the extra mile to ensure that they are satisfied with your work.

• Network with other EV technicians. One of the best ways to learn and stay up-to-date on the latest EV technology is to network with other EV technicians. You can do this by joining online forums, attending industry events, and connecting with other EV technicians on social media.

The Future of EV Technology

What does the future hold for EV technology? Here are some of the key trends that we can expect to see in the coming years:

• Battery technology: EV batteries are constantly improving, with new chemistries and designs offering higher energy density, faster charging, and longer lifespans. This will make EVs more affordable, practical, and appealing to a wider range of consumers.

• Charging infrastructure: The charging infrastructure for EVs is also rapidly expanding, with new public and private chargers being installed all the time. This will make it easier and more convenient for people to charge their EVs, regardless of where they live or work.

• Vehicle technology: EV manufacturers are also developing new technologies to improve the performance and efficiency of their vehicles. This includes things like more powerful electric motors, more aerodynamic designs, and lighter materials.

• Software: Software is also playing an increasingly important role in EVs. EV manufacturers are developing new software systems to control everything from the battery management system to the infotainment system. This software can help to improve the overall performance and experience of owning and driving an EV.

Some specific examples of EV technologies that we might see in the near future include:

• Solid-state batteries: Solid-state batteries are a new type of battery that offers a number of advantages over traditional lithium-ion batteries, including higher energy density, faster charging, and longer lifespans. Solid-state batteries are still in the early stages of development, but they have the potential to revolutionize the EV industry.

• Wireless charging: Wireless charging would make it even more convenient to charge an EV, as there would be no need to plug in a cable. Wireless charging technologies are still in their early stages of development, but they have the potential to become mainstream in the future.

• Vehicle-to-grid (V2G) technology: V2G technology would allow EVs to feed electricity back into the grid, which could help to balance the grid and reduce reliance on fossil fuels. V2G technology is still in its early stages of development, but it has the potential to play an important role in the future energy system.

EV technology is advancing rapidly. With new innovations being developed all the time, EVs are becoming more affordable, practical, and appealing to a wider range of consumers. In the coming years, we can expect to see EVs become more mainstream and play an increasingly important role in the global transportation system.

Resources for EV Technicians

EV technicians have access to a variety of resources that can help them learn, grow, and succeed in their careers. These resources include:

• Training programs: EV technician training programs are offered by a variety of sources, including community colleges, technical schools, private companies, and vehicle manufacturers. These programs can teach you the skills and knowledge you need to work on EV vehicles, including battery technology, electric motors, power electronics, and EV safety.

• Certifications: There are a number of EV technician certifications available from professional organizations and vehicle manufacturers. Getting certified can help you demonstrate your skills and knowledge to potential employers and customers. Some popular EV technician certifications include:

o   ASE L3 Hybrid/Electric Vehicle Specialist

o   NETA Level 1 and Level 2 Technician Certifications

o   Tesla START Certification

•   Online resources: There are a number of online resources available to EV technicians, including articles, videos, and tutorials. These resources can help you learn about the latest EV technologies and stay up-to-date on industry trends. Some popular online resources for EV technicians include:

o   EVTV

o   EV Training Lab

o   EV Pro Plus

•   Industry organizations: There are a number of industry organizations that support EV technicians. These organizations offer a variety of resources, such as training programs, networking opportunities, and job postings. Here are a few examples of industry organizations that support EV technicians:

o   National Electric Vehicle Technicians Association (NETA)

o   Electric Vehicle Association (EVA)

o   Society of Automotive Engineers (SAE)

In addition to these resources, many EV manufacturers offer their own training programs and certification programs for their technicians. You can also find a wealth of information about EV technology and repair on the websites of EV manufacturers and suppliers. There are specific ways in which EV technicians can benefit from these resources:

- A new EV technician can enroll in a training program to learn the basics of EV technology and repair.

- An experienced EV technician can get certified to demonstrate their skills and knowledge to potential employers and customers.

- An EV technician can read online articles and watch videos to stay up-to-date on the latest EV technologies.

- An EV technician can attend industry events and network with other EV technicians to learn new things and find job opportunities.

By taking advantage of these resources, EV technicians can stay ahead of the curve and prepare themselves to take advantage of the opportunities coming their way.

Becoming an EV technician is a challenging but rewarding career. With the right skills and knowledge, you can have a successful career in this growing industry.

I wish you the best of luck in your new career as an EV service technician!

ABOUT THE AUTHOR

Ronin C. Abel is an EV enthusiast who lives in New York City. He has a passion for EVs and their benefits for the environment, society, and economy. In this book, he introduces you to the world of EVs and shows you why he believes that becoming an EV service technician is a wonderful career choice at a time when the demand for EV servicing and maintenance is both lucrative and promising.

www.ingramcontent.com/pod-product-compliance
Lightning Source LLC
Chambersburg PA
CBHW050817260726
48660CB00004B/1478